Running in Circles

Running in Circles

How to Find Freedom from Addictive Behavior

Gary Steven Shogren
and Edward T. Welch

Strategic Christian Living series

Baker Books

A Division of Baker Book House Co
Grand Rapids, Michigan 49516

©1995 by Gary Steven Shogren and Edward T. Welch

Published by Baker Books
a division of Baker Book House Company
P.O. Box 6287, Grand Rapids, MI 49516-6287

Printed in the United States of America

Library of Congress Cataloging-in-Publication Data

Shogren, Gary Steven.
  Running in circles : how to find freedom from addictive behavior /
Gary Steven Shogren with Edward T. Welch.
      p.   cm. — (Strategic Christian living series)
      Includes bibliographical references (p.   ).
      ISBN 0-8010-8387-7
      1. Compulsive behavior—Religious aspects—Christianity. 2. Self-
control—Religious aspects—Christianity. 3. Addicts—Religious life.
I. Welch, Edward T., 1953–   . II. Title. III. Series: Strategic Christian
living.
      BV4598.7.S56   1995
      248.8'6—dc20   95–92

This book is lovingly dedicated to my anonymous brothers, sisters, and friends.

We know each other only by first names, but our souls have touched.

Contents

Appendixes

Acknowledgments

This book has been a true community project. Ed Welch helped me connect my ideas together into a system. Among my friends and colleagues at Biblical Theological Seminary, Penny Orr gave me the idea for this topic, and proposed some important improvements along the way. Ed Saadi offered his valuable observations, as did Sherry Kull, Carol Cornish, John Franke, and all the Garibaldi's gang.

Hello, Henrys, and many thanks for your ideas. That goes double for all the folks at Penacook, especially the Overcomers. Thanks to every one of you Sellersville Monday-nighters; and to you, Dona, Diane, and Rosalie, for the way you demonstrate living Christianity.

Thanks, Ma, for your encouragement and for your sensitive insights into human nature.

My wife and sweetheart Karen has not only worked at my side through this and every project; she also bears with me as I try to put these ideas into practice, and for that I am ever grateful.

Gary Steven Shogren

9

1

A Kingdom of Slaves

How to Know If You're Enslaved

I saw also the dreadful fate of Tantalus, who stood in a lake that reached his chin. He was dying to quench his thirst, but could never reach the water, for whenever the poor creature stooped to drink, it dried up and vanished, so that there was nothing but dry ground.

—Odysseus' description of Hades,
from *The Odyssey of Homer*

It's a Tuesday night and there are about a hundred people hugging and talking, and I am sitting back row center on a metal folding chair, trying my best to look invisible. From my coat pocket I fish out a cough drop, a defense against the thick cigarette smoke. An open meeting of Alcoholics Anonymous is just coming to order. As it unfolds,

we clap when folks stand to report their two weeks of sobriety, one whole year, five years.

Here in small town Pennsylvania there is an A. A. meeting or two on every night of the week, and that's just the
drinkers. At other meetings, hundreds of my neighbors rise
and admit to all sorts of addictions: "I am a compulsive gambler," or overeater, or junkie.

If you want to see the face of addiction, just look around;
addicts look just like the range of ordinary people. At A. A.
I run into homemakers, teachers, truck drivers, retirees,
college students. They "used," but they also tried to hold
down a job and even turned up at church occasionally. They
had become experts at concealing their problem. Many
times they were the last ones to figure it out.

They may have gotten their start with an experiment or
two. Some chemical or activity seemed to make them wiser,
stronger, more confident, but it was a trap. Remember the
old ploy of the drug pusher? He gives you the first few "hits"
for next to nothing. But then his price goes up, and you are
compelled to pay it.

At the heart of every addiction is that tired old "bait-and-
switch" technique: you are offered freedom; you are given
slavery.

Slavery was legally abolished in the U. S. over a century
ago, due in no small part to the influence of *Uncle Tom's
Cabin* by Harriet Beecher Stowe. She graphically depicted
how "Massuh" could beat, maim, even kill his slaves. Hus-
bands and wives and children were torn from each other
and sold off.

Stowe could have been writing about addiction! Alcohol
kills, it ruins families, it destroys minds. But slavishly, the
drinker keeps turning back to the bottle for sustenance.

According to the Bible, the comparison between addiction and slavery is right on target. We can get so mixed up
in a behavior that we become held against our will.

I have the desire to do what is good, but I cannot carry it out. For what I do is not the good I want to do; no, the evil I do not want to do—this I keep on doing . . . [making me] a prisoner of the law of sin.[1]

We can start defining addiction with that truth: addiction is bondage.

ADDICTION is bondage . . .

But where does that leave you?

A while back you dabbled in something, it doesn't matter what, to smooth over the hard edges of your life, and now you can't do without it.

That bondage gets worse. With your growing *tolerance* you will discover that the "buzz" gets harder to find. Two doses will be needed where one used to do the trick. And you may experience *withdrawal symptoms* if you try to quit or cut back.

At this point your brain feels like it's been borrowed from a stranger, and you begin to wonder if you aren't crazy after all. The truth is that you have bartered away your freedom. You are stuck in a senseless cycle of using, feeling remorse, vowing to do better next time, and then going right back to it.

Maybe you go to a church where the concept of sin has not been abolished. Whenever the topic comes up, your mind flits to that habit of yours. How many more sermons must you endure in which you could swear the preacher is looking at you alone, on the verge of revealing your terrible secret?

Be assured that there are millions with the same worry; some of them are probably sitting in your church and feeling the same isolation.

People in Bondage
and Their Substance of Choice

Addicts are not numbers, they are people. Let's meet a few, and see how addiction pulled them in.

Ron, An Alcoholic*

Maybe you can relate to Ron. Through all the stages of his life—school, blooming career, marriage, fatherhood—alcohol has been the one constant. He started out with a sip behind the gym, and then the occasional beer with his teenage buddies. He could drink normally for awhile—say, taking a cold brew at the ball park. From there, a tall one helped him unwind after work. "It's just beer," he reckoned, "it's not like I'm popping pills." Today Ron is drinking alone; in fact, he likes to drink by himself, where his wife won't get after him. Beer no longer takes him far enough fast enough, and a jolt of vodka won't be smelled on his breath. Sure, he has tried to set limits for himself—nothing before noon, never while driving, not in front of the kids—but he's broken them one by one. The problems he now faces at work and at home only make him think of drinking more—to "show them," or to take a vacation for a few minutes. Ron's whole life is rearranging itself around the bottle. Although he may go on the wagon once in a while, Ron is addicted to alcohol.

The Pull of Addiction

Ron has plenty of company. It's hard to medically distinguish the alcoholic from the problem drinker, but if they're all added up, the tally is 15.3 million in the United States alone. Alcohol takes second place to cigarettes (46.3 million users), a substance that leads to over 400,000 premature deaths annually (Wright 1994, 219–20). Compulsive gamblers are multiplying so quickly that statistics are hard to calculate; one standard estimate is that four percent of the adult population are problem gamblers, easily outnumbering the four million heavy users of illegal drugs (Berger 1992, 15).

Hold on a minute! Can gambling be an addiction when it doesn't involve a chemical substance? Yes; it all depends on what a thing does for you and what you do with it.

> Although there are many kinds of addiction, no matter what the addiction is, every addict engages in a relationship with an object or event in order to produce a desired mood change (Nakken 1988, 4).

For years people have argued over whether marijuana is physically addictive, or whether its pull is "merely" psychological.

ADDICTION is bondage to the rule of a substance, activity, or state of mind . . .

For our purposes it doesn't matter, since it yields a predictable "desired mood change." Exercise releases the body's natural painkillers, known as endorphins, producing a natural "high" that can be addictive. While anger is usually unpleasant, that biochemical rush can hook some people.

You can get hooked on all kinds of things, but these are some popular ones today:

Alcohol
Anger
Caffeine
Chocolate

Cocaine and other drugs
Eating disorders: bingeing, bingeing and purging (bulimia), self-starvation (anorexia)
Controlling others
Exercise
Fantasizing
Fears
Gambling, whether legal or illegal
Lying
Neatness or messiness
Nicotine
Nose drops
Pornography
Prescription drugs
Sex of all sorts, including masturbation and fantasy
Shoplifting
Shopping
Sleep
Sleep aids
Soft drinks
Sports (viewing or participating)
Sugar and sweets
TV
Violence
Work

Clearly not everyone who uses, say, chocolate is an addict. So how can we tell when the line has been crossed between free choice and slavery? One sign is that the addict keeps at it even after the bad consequences outweigh the supposed benefits.

It's just like when a kid scrapes his knee, and a scab forms. Still, he keeps picking at it. When his parents demand why he cannot leave it be, he has no answer; perhaps it gives him a feeling of control. Addicts, too, make irrational choices, for they are operating at a level where logic and common sense do not reach. They keep picking at it, in secret if they have to.

Sue, A Compulsive Shopper

There's nothing wrong with browsing, but Sue haunts the malls, buying clothes, shoes, appliances, gadgets—anything and everything—spending hundreds, thousands. On her last outing she bought her second diningroom set this year; four pairs of sale shoes, all black, all the wrong size; a figurine to put on her already-crowded piano; and some leftover Valentine's Day decorations at half off. "Wouldn't mother just love this little table for her hallway," she thinks, and buys two. The gift may pacify her after Sue wheedles yet another loan. Sue hasn't discovered the world of shopping by TV, and she doesn't hoard all her purchases. Tomorrow she will endure the humiliation of facing the sales clerk with her returns, and she may don a wig and dark glasses. For today, however, she has gotten her high. Later on, when she's exhausted and depressed, she'll lift her spirits with another spree.

Sue's husband, Carl, cannot begin to guess why she acts this way. He reasons, cajoles, pleads, loses his temper, cuts up the credit cards, sets up a budget, shows more affection, threatens to leave; but he cannot reach her. Ironically, Carl is out of control, too.

Carl, A Compulsive Overeater

Remember the old gibe, "Do you eat to live or live to eat?" Like most Americans, Carl likes his food, but overeating has come to dominate his life. He's the big guy you see at the steak house, moving through the buffet line with a towering plate in each hand, but who reasons that he is okay as long as he leaves the desserts alone. When they have friends to dinner, he hopes they don't polish off that nice casserole, and he can hardly wait until they leave so he can claim the leftovers. His trips to the convenience store "to get milk" turn into a snack safari. Carl hates being 70 pounds overweight, and he may blame his glands or his genes, but the fact is he just likes to eat. He figures that a man who works as hard as he does needs to keep up his strength. Of course, he's tried every imaginable diet and gimmick, and he's lost weight on them, but he always goes back to compulsive eating.

On top of all this, Carl's eating and Sue's shopping get intertwined—they make each other so upset by their compulsions that they turn to food or shopping in order to cope.

How Do You Know If You're Enslaved?

Let's draw up some probing questions that would help us to determine whether people like Ron, Sue, and Carl are addicted. Why not try them out on yourself? You might also get a close friend or family member to answer them about you.

1. Do family members or friends complain about you using it?
2. Have you repeatedly tried to quit, only to do it again?
3. Do you use any occasion—tension, fatigue, happy or sad feelings—to turn to it?
4. Do you ever hide it or sneak around with it?
5. Do you look forward to when you can get alone by yourself so that you can use it?
6. Do you find your mind wandering to it at odd times?
7. Do you have a ready set of excuses for why you use it?
8. Have you lost a job or run into friction at work over it?

9. Have you ever had to argue that you are not addicted to it?
10. Have you ever said "just once more won't hurt"?
11. After you use it, are you ashamed of yourself?
12. Have you ever lied about how often or how much you use it?
13. Do you avoid certain types of people, because of how they would react to you using it?
14. Do you keep comparing yourself with others who use it more than you do?
15. Are you ever conscious of God's disapproval when you use it?

ADDICTION is
bondage to the rule of a substance,
activity, or state of mind
which then becomes
the center of life . . .

If you can answer "yes" to *any* of these questions, then you may have crossed the line into addiction. For you, it is no longer an issue of choosing an activity or substance to help you cope. Your "drug" is becoming the center of your existence. Like Tantalus, you gulp at what you think you want, but you remain forever thirsty.

The Resemblances among Addiction's Slaves

Ron is hooked on a recreational substance (alcohol), Carl on an essential substance (food), Sue on an activity (shopping), but their behavior is similar. Addicts are inclined to act in certain ways.

Rationalizing

The gift of ignoring the obvious seems to cling to the addict. Sue spends less than she intended and claims to have "saved" money. Carl believes the half-truth, "I put nothing harmful into my mouth." Ron likes to say that "everyone has a little something to get him through the day." The problems caused by addiction are blamed on the family, the job, the government.

"Terminal Uniqueness"

"I'm not like other guys who drink," claims Ron. Addicts see themselves as special cases. Carl may see another man his size and wonder why he won't exercise a little more self-control, like Carl does. And because he is possessed by the feeling of "terminal uniqueness," he finds it hard to relate to the family, the church, or any group.

Deception

Secretive, sneaky, and devious; that's the addict. Compulsive gamblers hide the ticket stubs in the glove compartment or under the socks. They may visit a whole circuit of convenience stores, even buying something else to make it look as if the lottery ticket were an afterthought. The pornography is mailed under a plain wrapper, the shoplifted clothes are thrown away, the candy wrappers are neatly folded. Carl kids himself when he buys food with "half the calories missing!"—and wolfs down four times his normal amount.

And addicts try to beguile others, too. The woman with the broken leg comes to rely on prescribed painkillers, and lies about her level of pain in order to get more. She has her doctor's receptionist contact a different pharmacy for the next bottle, while letting the first pharmacist give her a refill too.

Let's drop in on Ron to see how he plays the game of "Deception." After work, he swings by Happy Harry's for a bump, then comes home to face the music from his wife Joan: "Did you stop by the bar on the way home?" The direct approach looks too painful for Ron, so he sorts through which card to play:

1. The Outright Lie: "I did not."
2. Word Games: "I did not stop by the bar." Meanwhile he reasons that, well, Happy Harry's is more like a pub than a bar; or that he did not stop BY it, but AT it.
3. The Defensiveness Defense: "Will you gimme a break from this constant nagging!"
4. The Counterattack: "Look—when I come home to a clean house and a hot meal, then you can worry about what I'm up to!"
5. The Delaying Tactic: "Can't talk now . . . " (he'll need to invent some emergency—have to use the bathroom, the car is making a funny noise).
6. The Technical Truth: "I did not stop at the bar," when in fact he stopped at the package store and had a drink in the car. A lie is not always limited to saying what is untrue; it may also involve NOT saying what IS true.
7. The Crossed Fingers: He says, "I did not go to the bar," but in his mind Ron will qualify himself: "Ah, but I did go the bar . . . There, I didn't exactly lie, did I?"
8. The Camouflage: Ron might pop a breath mint, or call to say he had to work late, or speed home so it looked like he didn't stop, or go around the block so that it appears he's coming from the opposite direction of the bar.

These tactics are by no means outlandish; in fact, a practiced alcoholic would consider them the work of an amateur.

Isolation

With so much energy and time devoted to the lie, addicts are typically washouts at human relationships. They find ways to dodge certain social situations: the family party; the long conversation; the class reunion. Vacations lose their appeal when that special treat won't fit into the suitcase. And how can Sue have any decent friendships when her true friend is shopping?

Ron early came to appreciate the effect that a few drinks had on his personality: no longer tongue-tied, he was the hit of every party. Years later, his drinking is no longer so charming—he is an abusive drunk, a good guy to avoid. Though he can be polite when he wants to be, Ron's philosophy of human relationships is summed up in one shameful credo: "To hell with all of you!" Ron senses the vacuum, and drinks to kill the pain of loneliness.

The Illusion of Self-Control

An addiction is not easily mastered, but addicts seek desperately to regain control. Here are some of their often paradoxical strategies:

> Drinkers: "I'll drink only beer, never drink alone, never drink with others, never drink before noon, never have it in the home, only drink in the home, promise to quit if it affects job performance, drink only if the job gives too much pressure, etc."

> Compulsive Neateners: "I'll clean the desk only once a week, never pick up after another, wipe the kitchen counter no more than once an hour, let spills stay on the floor at least 30 seconds before mopping."

Moderation is a virtue, but when addicts slow down or quit cold turkey, they crave the substance/activity even

more keenly. (Don't forget those "withdrawal symptoms"!)
Thus they set themselves up for the next fall.

ADDICTION is
bondage to the rule of a substance,
activity, or state of mind,
which then becomes
the center of life,
defending itself against the truth . . .

What these tricks have in common is that they are all defenses against the truth. The first job of your new overlord is to pass itself off as harmless. The popular label for that activity is "denial."

Truth, the Source of Hope

You may need hospitalization, treatment, or counseling in order to start over without your substance, but no program will fix your life. At the heart of every addiction is a lie, a world replete with subterfuge, fantasy, and delusion. In the face of the lie, truth is our best weapon.

The Truth about Addiction

The pursuit of truth is supposed to be a main occupation of Christianity, but you might imagine that the Bible is concerned only with "religious truth." In point of fact, it contains the truth that Ron, Sue, and Carl need. First, it gives an accurate picture of addiction; second, it explains why addiction happens and what it ultimately means; third, it lays out a clear, workable solution. Now is a good time to show its relevance in describing the problem of substance abuse.

In biblical times alcohol was the main addictive chemical, but what is said of alcohol abuse can be transferred to other substances.

> Who has woe? Who has sorrow?
> Who has strife? Who has complaints?
> Who has needless bruises? Who has bloodshot eyes?
>
> Those who linger over wine,
> who go to sample bowls of mixed wine.
>
> Do not gaze at wine when it is red,
> when it sparkles in the cup,
> when it goes down smoothly!
> In the end it bites like a snake
> and poisons like a viper.
> Your eyes will see strange sights
> and your mind imagine confusing things.
> You will be like one sleeping on the high seas,
> lying on top of the rigging.
> "They hit me," you will say, "but I'm not hurt!
> They beat me, but I don't feel it!
> When will I wake up
> so I can find another drink?"[2]

Now, the Bible speaks in nontechnical language, but notice the precision with which it describes compulsive drinking, craving, delusions, hallucinations, mental confusion, loss of equilibrium, "feeling no pain" after a beating (or is it "denial"?), and that irrational urge for more.

People commonly misapply this text, passing it off as the Bible's *solution* to chemical dependency. But nothing could be further from the truth! It is given as a *prevention* to alcohol abuse: don't get hooked in the first place, or these things will happen to you! Nevertheless, when we come to consider the Bible's explanation of addiction in the next chapter, keep in mind that it scored a direct hit in describing its symptoms.

The Truth about You and Your Problem

A conspiracy of silence may help addicts to justify their pain, but it will never do for someone who wants change. Face your own situation squarely! Admit that you have made a muddle of your life, and that your substance has thrown you into turmoil.

The Truth about God

I believe that God exists and that he is in charge. If this is true, it follows that his view of things is the one that ultimately matters. But we humans like to view the world in terms of how things affect "Me." Oh, granted, you are hammered by substance abuse—you are plagued by anxiety, sleeplessness, debt, delusion, and rejection. From a human-centered viewpoint (the fancy word is "anthropocentric" viewpoint) we might come to the conclusion that "we're only hurting ourselves." If we are a bit more altruistic we might grant that we hurt other people, too.

Anthropocentric Worldview— a human- or self-centered view of the universe

But what about God? The Twelve Steps, foundation of Alcoholics Anonymous and other programs, promise that "a Power greater than ourselves could restore us to sanity" and that he is happy to help us if we just ask.

This is positive, but if this is all we believe, then the Higher Power seems a bit passive about human affairs. The God who is described in the Bible grieves when his standards are rejected, and he actively pursues people seeking their return to him. And we are told that the God of the Bible, and he alone, exists.

> But the LORD [Hebrew "Yahweh"] is the true God; he is the living God, the eternal King.[3]

That name, "Living God," reflects his Hebrew name, Yahweh, which means "He Who Is" or "The Existing One." And according to the Bible, the God who really exists is more than a smiling benevolence.

> See to it, brothers, that none of you has a sinful, unbelieving heart that turns away from the living God. . . . It is a dreadful thing to fall into the hands of the living God.[4]

In the God-centered (or "theocentric") universe described in the Bible, every one of your actions matters with God, particularly when you turn to some substance as your master. We must start our program with God and not with our own desires or needs.

Theocentric Worldview— A God-centered view of the universe.

Our definition of addiction must include God, or else it is deficient. But quoting Bible verses and putting God into the equation will not be enough to build a God-centered approach. For addiction does not simply *lead to* estrangement from God's kingdom—rather, our problems also *begin* with alienation from God, and addiction is a symptom of that broken relationship. Thus, one more phrase should give us a full definition of addiction:

***ADDICTION is
bondage to the rule of a substance,
activity, or state of mind,
which then becomes
the center of life,
defending itself from the truth,
and leading to estrangement
from God's kingdom.***

If we don't close this chapter, we can't begin our scrutiny of the spiritual causes of addiction. But let's not end on a dismal note. If you take nothing else from this chapter, let it be that the God of the Bible, the Living God, is the God of hope. In God's mighty kingdom you will find the hope of true liberation.

> Why are you downcast, O my soul?
> Why so disturbed within me?
> Put your hope in God,
> for I will yet praise him,
> my Savior and my God.[5]

***Arising out of our alienation
from the Living God,
addiction is
bondage to the rule of a substance,
activity, or state of mind,
which then becomes
the center of life,
defending itself from the truth,
and leading to further estrangement
from God's kingdom.***

ASSIGNMENTS

1. Make a list of ways you have covered up your guilty secret. Have you lied? hidden things? rationalized? made excuses? isolated yourself from others? Keep the list with you for a few days and add to it things that come to mind.

2. Lying may take many forms. Look up these verses from Proverbs: 6:12–19; 10:9–10; 11:9; 12:19–22; 19:5; 20:17; 21:6; 26:18–19. Do they uncover other ways in which you have neglected the truth? What are the results of falsehood?

3. Read through Luke 15. God the father is symbolized by three characters: a shepherd, a woman, a father. He is the kind of God who searches for lost people (sheep, coin) and gladly welcomes them back into his presence (runaway boy). How do these pictures of God relate to you in your present state? What do they say about God's active work to recover you and bring you home?

Introductory quotation: Homer 1944, 145.

2

The Real Nature
of the Kingdom of Slaves

Disease, Low Self-Esteem, or What?

Man is one of your creatures, Lord, and his instinct is to
praise you. . . . The thought of you stirs him so deeply that
he cannot be content unless he praises you, because you
have made us for yourself and our hearts find no peace until
they rest in you.

—Augustine, *Confessions*

Addicts are endlessly annoyed by well-meaning people
who tell them to "just exercise a little self-control." But in
fact, they too puzzle over why they are the way they are.
Am I sick? a sinner? misunderstood? crazy? deprived? depraved? none of the above, all of the above?

The book *Alcoholics Anonymous* (nicknamed the Big
Book) reminds the drinker that alcohol is "cunning, baf-

fling, powerful" (A. A. World Service 1976, 58–59). Your habit keeps you in its dark kingdom, partly by keeping you in confusion. To be free you have to know the nature of that prison. Let's look first at the "disease model" of addiction, and second, at the issue of self-esteem. We will then explore how addiction is related to the "Big Questions," like the one about why we exist in the first place.

Is Addiction a Disease?

Baseball's "Charlie Hustle," Pete Rose, couldn't outrun the fallout from his compulsive gambling. In 1989 his secret world fell apart, as the press revealed the extent of his massive betting sprees (at times, $2000 to $5000 for a single game). In the end, gambling cost him his one great love—baseball.

Rose was jailed for tax evasion. But many said that since he had the disease of compulsive gambling, he ought to be given treatment, not punishment. You might as well spank a child for having a toothache! In this pop version of the "disease model" the addict is not accountable for his or her behavior. Addiction is not just *like* a disease, or *best treated* as a disease—it *is* a disease, and the sufferer is not responsible for having it.

A more balanced version of the disease model was adopted by Alcoholics Anonymous (A. A.) in the 1930s: some people seem to have an abnormal reaction to alcohol and are unable to judge when they have had enough. When sober, they forget their trouble with drink, and become obsessed with taking another (A. A. World Service 1976, xxiii–xxx). One recent book concurs with the traditional A. A. version: "Labeling addictions as 'disease' does not absolve you of responsibility for your behavior, for decisions that affect your life, or for the consequences of over- or undertreating yourself" (Wilson and Wilson 1992, 115).

But that theory has been twisted into an excuse for all sorts of behavior.

> In 1980, a data processor for the Philadelphia School District was fired for being late to work virtually every day he was on the job. He sued, claiming that chronic lateness should be considered a disability. A Pennsylvania Court of Common Pleas agreed with him, citing the Pennsylvania Human Relations Act (Sykes 1992, 130–31).

How many times have you heard of some great wickedness—mass murder, cannibalism, torture—and you've heard it said, "That person is sick!" But now imagine every evil deed being labeled a symptom of some disease or another. Whole families can be sick or "dysfunctional," and counseling is transmuted into "therapy" (from the Greek *therapeia*, "healing").

We're trying to view the universe as God-centered. If addiction is the route that much evil takes, and if the Living God despises evil, then we must deal with the question, "How does God view the relationship between evil and addiction?" The answer lies in the Bible's teaching about human depravity.

If we read a newspaper exposé about a producer of child pornography, I may turn to you and say that he's "depraved." But when a theologian says that we're *all* depraved, the word takes on a different cast: it is the moral ruin of the whole person, which makes us fall short of God's standards, and in turn motivates us to sin further against God.

Our experience, we are taught, is determined by the experience of Adam long ago, and his fall into sin.

> Therefore, just as sin entered the world through one man, and death through sin, and in this way death came to all men, because all sinned . . .[1]

It's as if Adam were standing at the precipice of a long, steep slope that is covered with slippery mud and without a handhold. He had the freedom to choose to step off the edge, and in fact he did so when he first rebelled against God. But now he finds that he cannot choose to be back at the top. The more he tries to improve his position, the more muddied and stained he becomes.

That's the dilemma we are in today: born to die, and without the option of choosing whether we want to be sinners. About the only choice we have outside of Christ is over what sort of sinner we will be. Some of us will express our inner pollution through random sins, while others will be drawn to patterns of sin, or addiction.

We might illustrate the work of depravity in this way: in 1980, newly married, I suddenly developed a terrible headache and a fever. I was hospitalized, and it turned out that viral meningitis had inflamed the meninges, membranes that surround the brain and spinal cord. When my wife asked if it was catching, the doctor said, "Sure, but the virus that did this might just give you a sore throat. It just happens that this time it infected this certain membrane."

Sin is not a disease! But like that virus, it can produce different symptoms throughout the population: one person is a miser, another a big spender; one a sanctimonious churchgoer, another an upright atheist.

Do you see what this means for addiction? Alcoholism has its own warning signs, but it's caused by the same bug that draws people into compulsive gambling, habitual violence, or even the occasional "white lie." They are expressions of the systematic failure that is shared by all.

But hasn't science proven that certain people drink because of their genes? No! The bottom line in scientific research is that genes do not force people to be alcoholics. For example, we know that the majority of children of drinking parents do not themselves drink heavily. If there is an inherited tendency to alcoholism, then personal choices and other factors (peer pressure, home environment, availability of the substance) will still go in to the final determination of who gets hooked.

Well, if it is not inherited, then perhaps addiction is an environmental disease: child molesters come from dysfunctional backgrounds, thieves are reacting to poverty, and so forth. In a new version of "the devil made me do it," fingers are pointed at society.

Of course, environment will have some effect on our habits. For example, an Englishman of the fifteenth century could hardly have become addicted to tobacco, as it had not yet been introduced to Europe. A widow within a bus ride of Atlantic City is more likely to gamble than her counterpart elsewhere.

But you don't really want to embrace the philosophy of "determinism," blaming your failures (and successes!) on something outside yourself. Even if that were possible, it would render your choices truly meaningless. In most circumstances, you agree with the Bible that individuals should be held responsible for their actions . . . especially when someone dents your fender!

So how do our thoughts on the disease model and moral responsibility help, for example, a compulsive spender? Let's say that Sue finally "hits bottom" and heads out to Debtors Anonymous, where she concludes that

> It doesn't matter how it happened—too many sales in my town at one time, or once too often I turned to shopping when I was blue. What matters now is that I admit that I have a problem, and that I am responsible to not shop compulsively.

But the Bible goes beyond the Debtors Anonymous model, informing Sue that she is responsible in God's eyes for turning to her "drug" again and again until she was hooked. She needs to admit that her growing dependence was her way of rejecting him.

Is Addiction Due to Low Self-Esteem?

From the psychologist's office to the TV talk show, it is "known" that addiction is caused by low self-esteem. Well, Sue certainly does seem to be down on herself.

> No matter what I do, I can't please my parents or my husband, Carl. I can't balance the checkbook or cook nice meals or land a good job. I'm not talented in music or crafts like the other ladies in church, and I never will be.

Compulsive shopping makes her feel special; no one can sniff out a bargain like she can! And so it might appear to be a simple case of cause and effect: if a poor self-image causes her to shop compulsively, then raising her self-image should return her to normal.

But wait! Cause and effect are not always as simple as they appear! For example, it seems as if every time I sit down to do some writing, the telephone rings. Maybe one day I'll put my index finger into the air and say, "Aha! switching on my word processor must cause that annoying ringing noise!" Add the human element, and cause and effect are not straightforward. Sue's problems started on a day that the whole world seemed to be against her. She shopped, but inevitably she felt lower than before. So what came first, low self-esteem or compulsive shopping?

And even if we describe how Sue feels, have we explained what's really going on? It may surprise you that nowhere does the Bible commend high self-esteem. If anything, it regards self-love as a fault.

> People will be *lovers of themselves*, lovers of money, boastful, *proud*, abusive, disobedient to their parents, ungrate-

ful, unholy, *without love*, unforgiving, slanderous, without self-control, brutal, not lovers of the good, treacherous, rash, *conceited*, lovers of pleasure rather than lovers of God—having a form of godliness but denying its power. Have nothing to do with them.[2]

Today's apostles of self-esteem exaggerate the alternatives: "The church used to teach me to think of myself as worthless; but the truth is, God made me, and God don't make no junk."

Do you see how the focus here is not on God, but on "Me"? God is brought into the picture to prove my worth. But remember we live in a world that is made by God for his pleasure! In that theocentric world, addiction is the vandalism of God's workmanship.

Nowhere in the Bible does God tell us to love ourselves; when it says to "love your neighbor as yourself" it assumes that you love yourself already. But you wonder, how is that possible for people who do self-destructive things, such as shooting heroin? Well, the Bible shows us that love is not always a nice feeling, but a pattern of actions. And so, yes, heroin addicts do love themselves, so much so that they will give themselves whatever they want, no matter who gets hurt.

God's greatest desire is that you should "love the Lord your God with all your heart and with all your soul and with all your mind and with all your strength."[3] And so we must fall in love, not with ourselves, but with our maker.

The Roots of Addiction in Our Reason for Being

The French have a phrase for it: *raison-d'être*, or reason for being. Do you know why you exist? Is it to make money, have fun, live for yourself, live for others?

Take another look at the quotation that begins this chapter. Way back in the fourth century A.D., Augustine lived his life for himself. After years of this, he came to realize that all his gifts—including a solid education and a powerful mind—made sense only through the God who created him.

The oft-quoted passage of the Westminster Shorter Catechism puts it just right:

> What is the chief end of man [i.e., his reason for being]?
> Man's chief end is to glorify God, and to enjoy him forever.

"Man is by his constitution a religious animal," said Edmund Burke. A dog can be taught to hold its paws together, close its eyes, and make dog noises in a parody of prayer. But only human beings can relate to God as persons to a person. People, not animals, can bring him glory by their own choice.

But our three friends are drifting in the opposite direction. Little by little, Ron lives to drink, Sue to shop, Carl to eat. Their whole *raison-d'être* is swallowed up by their foolish choices and later by their feebleness in making choices. All three are living as animals, throwing away God's purpose for creating them.

> So God created man in his own image, in the image of God he created him; male and female he created them.[4]

The Bible reveals that God made Adam and Eve "in his image," with the capacity to worship him and have fellowship with him. When they worshiped God, they also celebrated their role as his image-bearers.

So . . . how did we get from there to here? What in the world went wrong? Theologians describe the event with an ominous-sounding label: "the Fall."

Sadly, many people regard the story of the Fall in Genesis 3 as a myth, when the Bible presents it as a straightforward explanation for the mess we're in: Adam and Eve were enjoying their *raison-d'être* as creatures who loved their Creator. The only restriction that God gave them was to avoid eating the fruit from one tree, the Tree of the Knowledge of Good and Evil.

Satan dangled some bait before them: With the knowledge that this fruit would give, they would be as gods themselves, free from the yoke of God's kingdom. So our first parents decided to gamble with being the masters of their own fate. What they got in the end was not emancipation but enslavement.

But did their natural drive for worship just get shut off? Hardly!

From science fiction we get the story formula of the robot whose makers have long since departed. The machine is programmed for a function, and it is found centuries later, mindlessly performing actions that no longer have any purpose.

We are not robots! But since the fall, men and women have rambled along, worshiping, worshiping, worshiping, looking for some power greater than themselves. They chisel gods out of stones, metal, logs, people, or pump themselves full of biochemicals and drugs in a pathetic effort to satisfy their deepest and most human drive: the need to serve God. And that, folks, makes religion the most natural of human productions, for a reason revealed in Bob Dylan's music: "You gotta serve somebody."

Addicts talk about their compulsions in many ways: you commonly hear about "an itch that can't be scratched" or "a void that can't be filled." One recent writer says

> We must therefore understand what all addictions and the process of all addictions have in common: the out of control and aimless searching for wholeness, happiness, and peace through a relationship with an object or event (Nakken 1988, 4).

From a theocentric viewpoint, Augustine diagnosed the problem as a deep restlessness that could only be eased in

God himself. Even addiction is a method for ignoring our need of God, a way of telling him, "I'll get back to you later." Addicts try to play god, deciding when they will feel "up," or "down," or whatever, so long as its a state of their own choosing. With the substance, they feel temporarily in charge, powerful, and fulfilled. But it also makes them grab even harder for control. Thus, the heroin addict beats his children for making noise and annoying him. The guilt that comes the morning after is quickly assuaged with more chemicals. Human laws that forbid his substance are "stupid" when applied to him, he fails at his job because the boss is out to get him, religion is for weaklings. He insists, "I know what I'm doing!"

And so one way of looking at addiction, let's say alcoholism, is this: an alcoholic is a person who desperately yearns to be god—almighty, all-knowing, autonomous—and drinks to ease the disgrace of being merely a creature.

And yet . . .

. . . against every expectation, the Living God stepped in to recover alcoholics—yes, and junkies and the violent and the control freaks. If God has redeemed you, then "you are not your own; you were bought at a price. Therefore honor God with your body."[5] It is to God's loving and powerful rescue mission that we must turn next.

ASSIGNMENTS

1. Divide a page into three columns, labeled GOD, (your name), and SIN. Starting with the middle column, list every part of your life that you can think of: emotions, creativity, ambition, sexuality, sports, you name it. In the "God" column, write out how each of those words can be used to bring God pleasure. Now in the "Sin" column, list how each of those can be used for sin. Begin to see how badly sin can ruin you for your original purpose: to glorify God and to enjoy him forever.

2. List the ways in which you are responsible for being stuck in addiction. Did you choose to pick up that substance? Did you go against the advice of your parents or friends? Did you ignore what you knew to be true?

3. Study these verses on drunkenness—make a list of the symptoms of this behavior and find which ones are applicable to your problem: Prov. 20:1; 21:17; 23:19–21; 31:4–7; Isa. 28:1–8; Hab. 2:15–16.

Introductory quotation: Augustine 1961, 21.

3

Finding Freedom
in the Kingdom of God

Acting Out the Gospel

Jesus, Son of David, have mercy on me!

—Bartimaeus of Jericho, in the Gospel of Mark

Giving thanks to the Father, who has qualified you to share
in the inheritance of the saints in the kingdom of light. For
he has rescued us from the dominion of darkness, and has
brought us into the kingdom of the Son he loves, in whom
we have redemption, the forgiveness of sins.

—Paul 's Epistle to the Colossians

Ron has about had it with running in circles. He struggles, he makes promises, he swears he'll change—and time
after time he fails. He drinks to hide the failure from himself. But just suppose he gets so desperate that he looks for
some help from God.

Hey, great! you say. Isn't this the answer, to turn to God
for help?

Not exactly. Not in this case.

Ron is guessing that if God will just give him a boost, he'll be able to take it from there. And after this is licked, he promises himself, I'll shape up into a better person than I've been—so it's a win-win situation for God and me both!

The Living God Must Save Us from Ourselves

God will never help Ron win his independence. With him, the way of freedom is through unconditional surrender to his kingdom.

But Ron will put up with any number of indignities to avoid submitting to the Living God: he will retch, listen to people snicker behind his back, lose his job, live with a hellish home life, in short, lose his humanity—but he'd "feel silly" turning himself over completely to God.

Is God a crutch for the weak-minded? Hardly! God has so designed us that we must latch onto some god. What *is* a crutch, is having just any god for the sake of having one.

In Alcoholics Anonymous, drunks are urged to find some sort of Higher Power. They are told to add or subtract characteristics from their god until it feels right. This is fine, so long as one assumes that there is no Living God. But does anyone stop to think that such personal Higher Powers do not exist outside of the imagination?

- What if Ron comes to believe in an all-powerful God who will hold individuals accountable for their deeds?
- And what if Mark, a buddy who is in A. A., comes to believe in an all-powerful Being who does not care about sin or evil, but is happy to help drunks?

According to the Bill of Rights, people are free to believe what they like, but Ron and Mark cannot both be correct about the Supreme Being. There can be no "my god" and "your god" unless there are two gods.

Now Ron and Mark at least believe in a Supreme Being. But what if you can't believe in any traditional deity? Some will simply define God as "*G*ood *O*rderly *D*irection." Many will come to regard the group itself as the Higher Power that can set them free, while a few will actually rely on a knob on the door of the meeting room. Often referred to by his (or her) initials, "H. P." is custom-tailored to meet the follower's felt needs: a doorknob is rarely demanding, and it can't zap you if you get out of line. In fact, if any god will do, then you could probably cope with no god at all.

The Living God
The God of the Bible
The God of Creation
The God and Father of our
Lord Jesus Christ

But remember what Augustine said: "*You* have made us for *yourself* and our hearts find no peace until they rest in *you.*" For Augustine, this God was no vague Higher Power. He had spent years searching for truth, first in Manicheanism, with its dual forces of good and evil, and then in neo-Platonism, with its God of cool reason. He eventually rejected these gods as false, and surrendered to the Living God whom his Christian mother worshiped. By "you" he means the God and Father of the Lord Jesus Christ, revealed to Augustine through the Bible.

Many would prefer a deity with fuzzier edges: good and caring, but not restricted to what the Bible says about him. But even pluralistic groups have limits to their tolerance—a Twelve-Step God, for example, cannot be harsh or judgmental. Apparently, if we must keep an open mind about God, he must be broad minded about us, despite biblical statements to the contrary. But just remember that we would not even know that "God is love" unless the Bible told us that!

I wish you could have met a group who once lived in northern Greece. Before Paul evangelized them, they had Higher Power aplenty, a whole pantheon of gods and goddesses, with one suitable for every taste. These figures were supposed to personify heaven's wisdom and power, but to Paul they were weak idols. The Thessalonians needed to turn to the Living God, the God who could rescue them through Jesus Christ.

> You turned to God from idols to serve *the living and true God*, and to wait for his Son from heaven, whom he raised from the dead—Jesus, who rescues us from the coming wrath.[1]

Idols may strike Westerners as a bit silly: people going around making statues in the forms of men and women, birds, animals, or fish, and calling them gods. But think it through: worshiping a crocodile is no more outlandish than trusting in a doorknob, or praying to that part of you that is a spark of the divine, and so making a god that looks just like you.

In chapter two we saw that, at heart, addiction is a spiritual breakdown. You don't want to build your own god now—that's what landed you in the kingdom of bondage in the first place! And no manmade god will ride to your rescue when you cry out for help.

Beyond that, never, never reduce Christ to being your Higher Power in the same way that Allah is the Muslim's Power or Shiva the Hindu's—just fill in the blank with the deity of your choice! Christ is the Lord of all, and God the only Living God in a field of impostors.

Enter the Cross as God's Solution

You may think of it mainly as a traditional symbol of Christianity, but the cross was God's forceful move to rescue people from the dark kingdom.

Down the road from the Thessalonians, the Corinthian Christians had been soundly changed by the gospel. In a letter written about five years later, Paul recalled their former lives.

> Do you not know that the wicked will not inherit the kingdom of God? Do not be deceived: Neither sexually immoral nor idolaters nor adulterers nor male prostitutes nor homosexual offenders nor thieves nor the greedy nor drunkards nor slanderers nor swindlers will inherit the kingdom of God. And that is what some of you were.[2]

Society pushes the idea that minor "sins" may be tidied up by religion, but pattern problems such as addiction are best left to the trained professional. But just look at that list . . . the Corinthians had every sort of problem pattern:

1. Sexually immoral—people who uncontrollably practice illicit sex of any form.
2. Idolaters—not just a religious option, it was a lifestyle. Idolaters transgress both the first and second of the Ten Commandments.
3. Adulterers—sex that violates the marriage covenant and the seventh commandment.
4. Male prostitutes—the word denotes either the passive homosexual partner, or a male homosexual prostitute. This word is paired with . . .
5. Homosexual offenders—someone who practices homosexual intercourse, perhaps the "active" partner.
6. Thieves—people steal for all sorts of reasons, but in so doing they break the eighth commandment of God.
7. Greedy—a craving to have another's possessions, in violation of the tenth commandment.
8. Drunkards—the drunkard engages in repeated intoxication, with its attendant loss of self-control.
9. Slanderers—people who habitually malign others.
10. Swindlers—those who practice deception so as to get gain.

The 10 Commandments

1. *You shall have no other gods
   before me.*

2. *You shall not make for yourself an idol
   in the form of anything in heaven above
   or on the earth beneath or in the waters
   below. You shall not bow down to them
   or worship them; for I, the Lord your
   God, am a jealous God . . .*

3. *You shall not misuse the name of the
   Lord your God.*

4. *Remember the Sabbath day by keeping
   it holy.*

5. *Honor your father and your mother.*

6. *You shall not murder.*

7. *You shall not commit adultery.*

8. *You shall not steal.*

9. *You shall not give false testimony
   against your neighbor.*

10. *You shall not covet anything that
    belongs to your neighbor.*

Have you noticed? Every type of person that Paul lists in this passage is practicing a vice as a way of life. And all of these lifestyle sins are addictive: the drunkard abuses a substance, and the others a habitual activity. Christ did not just save the Corinthians from their sins generally, he also delivered them from the sins by which they were identified in society (Philip is a male prostitute, Drusilla a swindler).

Paul's teaching will strike some as hopelessly unscientific: he would have God send people to hell for being "sick" with alcoholism. To hear others tell it, there is barely any point of contact whatever between "drunkard" and "alcoholic."

But let us first make sure we understand what Paul means by the word "drunkard."

(a) Perhaps he credits the gospel with changing problem drinkers, but not alcoholics.

. . . or (b) he is calling the predisposition to alcohol itself a sin against God.

. . . or (c) he is pointing to a specific behavior, that is, people who drink to harmful excess, regardless of whether or not they are addicted.

This last option is preferable: the word by definition points to a behavior, not its underlying motivation. Paul would be listing drunkenness as an offense against God, whether it happens once or chronically, and this squares with the rest of the Bible's teaching against all intoxication: "Do not get drunk on wine, which leads to debauchery."[3] Christ saved people who had drinking problems of every sort . . . perhaps even those who did not exhibit any visible symptoms of inebriation:

The Corinthians changed their identity from "drunkards," "slanderers," and so forth to "saints." Paul continues

but you were washed, you were sanctified, you were justified in the name of the Lord Jesus Christ and by the Spirit of our God.[4]

Paul pulls out the strong Greek word for "but" *(alla)* to show the radical change they have undergone. Against all expectation, men and women trapped in lifestyle sins became washed (made clean from past filth), sanctified (made holy), and justified (declared to be right with God), and all of this through the cross.

> For I resolved to know nothing while I was with you except Jesus Christ and him crucified.[5]

For that reason I shudder when I hear Christians complain, "I went to the pastor for counseling about my problem, and all he did was quote Bible verses at me! Doesn't he realize that I need serious help?" It's always hard to tell who was at fault: maybe the counselee doesn't want to believe that Christ is king even over addictive substances; maybe the counselor doesn't take the time to show why and how it is true.

Nevertheless, it is in the cross that we find the true meaning of recovery: it is not that I recover, but that I *am recovered,* that God recovers the whole me through the cross. Christ did not merely give the Corinthians a nice religious experience, and then point them to a therapist to handle their "real" problems. If Christ cannot deliver you from alcohol or shoplifting, then he cannot deliver you from anything.

Now, if I were sitting where you're sitting, and I picked up a book written by a Christian, I'd expect to read that Christ is the only way out of addiction. Well, it may be risky to say this, but it is true:

> You do not need to turn to God or to Christ in order to quit your addictive substance or behavior.

Hey, don't look so shocked! Clearly, there are people who quit substance abuse while still atheists, agnostics, or pantheists. Just picture all those exhippies from the 1960s who are living respectable lives today—and not necessarily with Christ. And frankly, if people can abstain from compulsive sex by believing in a doorknob, then pretty much anything is possible. But does it make sense to try it apart from the Living God? Put yourself in this picture . . .

> A man goes overboard on a stormy sea. Although a rescue team comes and tosses him life rings and shouts at him to let himself be helped, he refuses. He struggles and exerts himself, and for hours he manages to tread water. Against all odds, for one day, for two, he spares his own life by his own power . . . when suddenly, in a flash, the sun goes nova, destroying him and all life on earth.

You too may work and sweat and somehow manage to keep your addiction at bay, maybe even for a lifetime, but you're going nowhere fast. The main point of the gospel is that you may get right with the God who made you and will judge you.

Well, that makes sense for the potential convert, but what if you're sure you are born again already? Even genuine Christians are open to addiction, as they turn their attention away from Christ alone and empower some idol in their lives. In fact, that seems to be the point of Paul's reminiscing with the Corinthians—he warns them about falling once again into sinful patterns, as a close look at 1 Corinthians 6:1–8 will reveal. So do the already converted miss out on the power of the gospel?

By no means!

Recovery from Rebellion
Is the Acting Out of the Gospel

If you need relief from pain, you can swallow an analgesic pill. Or you can rub an analgesic cream on an affected area, such as a bee sting, for topical relief. So too with the gospel: God has saved me, yet I am addicted to cigarettes; my obsession can be relieved by applying the gospel specifically to it.

In the Cross We Live "In Christ"

It is in Romans 6 that Paul handles an old question: If God accepts the wicked by faith, then doesn't the gospel rob people of any motivation to please God? After all, the church cannot threaten the undamned with damnation, so what keeps them from running amok?

That sort of thinking is all backwards, says Paul. We believers are "alive to God in Christ Jesus" (Rom. 6:11). We have "died to sin" (Rom. 6:2), with the goal that "we should no longer be slaves to sin" (Rom. 6:6). And all Christians have had that experience, whether or not they take advantage of it. The other side is that Christians still need to take decisive action against their inner tendency to sin. That constant tension between What Is and What Should Be comes up later on.

> In the same way, count yourselves dead to sin but alive to God in Christ Jesus. Therefore do not let sin reign in your mortal body so that you obey its evil desires [Note: "count" means "reckon it as true because it IS true"].[6]

There's that kingdom language again: "do not let sin reign." That despot used to tell us what to do and we had no choice but to yield. But Christ set us free from the "dominion of darkness" and brought us into submission to our rightful sovereign. How then, can sin dominate a person in Christ? By voluntarily surrendering, we can allow ourselves in practice to become slaves.

> Do not offer the parts of your body to sin, as instruments of wickedness. . . . Don't you know that when you offer

yourselves to someone to obey him as slaves, you are slaves to the one whom you obey—whether you are slaves to sin, which leads to death, or to obedience, which leads to righteousness.[7]

The apostle Peter makes a similar point: "a man is a slave to whatever has mastered him."[8]

Too often we think that the cross just redeems a bit of us known as the "soul," but in fact it brings a whole new life, a life of surrender. The element of surrender in the Twelve Steps was taken mainly from Romans 6; just look at Step Three.

[We] made a decision to turn our will and our lives over to the care of God as we understood Him.

Compare it with Paul's statement:

Offer yourselves to God, as those who have been brought from death to life; and offer the parts of your body to him as instruments of righteousness.[9]

But Romans 6 doesn't work unless you are first of all alive in Christ. Outside of Christ, you are in prison even now. Whether you are "using" or abstaining is only of secondary importance.

Let's stop and boil all this doctrine down to an outline.

1. *Outside of Christ*, men and women live as slaves to sin. Some people may be addicts, and others upstanding citizens, but they are all in bondage.
2. *At the point of conversion*, people are instantaneously released from sin's decisive control.
3. *In Christ*, they are subject to his kingdom, but they may become enmeshed again in slavery. They need

to surrender those specific parts that keep sliding into trouble.

Willpower Is Not Our Savior

How tragic when an addict turns to a gospel-preaching church for help, only to hear the tired old message, "It just takes a bit of willpower!" Even A. A.'s Big Book stresses that willpower is part of the problem.

> Selfishness—self-centeredness! That, we think, is the root of our troubles. . . . So our troubles, we think, are basically of our own making. They arise out of ourselves, and the alcoholic is an extreme example of self-will run riot, though he usually doesn't think so (A. A. World Service 1976, 62).

Does it even need to be pointed out that a gospel of self-control is NOT the gospel of Christ? No, physical exercise will not "cure" sexual addiction, nor will smaller helpings get you around an obsession with food. Grabbing for control of an addiction with more willpower is like trying to pick up Jello—it just slithers through your fingers, and the harder you try to clutch onto it, the faster it slips away. The real solution lies in surrender to the Living God.

Victory Is a Way of Life

It's a Sunday evening testimony service, and a brother stands up to say: "I was a drunk, but twenty years ago I gave my life to Christ. He changed me completely, and I've never taken a drink nor have I wanted one from that day on."

What a wonderful tribute to God's power! But you sit in your pew, trying to fit it all into your experience: Is this invariably the way God rescues us from addiction? If I am converted, and it then takes me many months of falling down and getting back up before victory comes, does that mean Christ is not in me?

Stop right where you are, please, and pay attention to this crucial bit of information:

> None of the Bible verses we have looked at guarantees you instant freedom from pattern sins and their temptations. In fact, there are none, period. I 've checked! Not a one.

Even the man who was instantaneously rescued from drink will probably tell you that he needs to live that victory every day, not just relive a memory from long ago. If he doesn't, he's probably practicing some other sort of addictive behavior in order to fill the gap.

This truth is so foundational: when I became a Christian, I entered into an in-between situation. I am washed, yet I can still get dirty. I stand in the kingdom of God, yet I feel myself slipping into the kingdom of bondage. I can choose to sin, and I can choose not to sin, and most days I do both. It's hurtful to God, but my spiritual journey will occasionally hit a pothole.

This is why it is wrong to promise people wholesale relief if they "just turn it over to God this very moment!" They may sincerely determine to relinquish their sin, and they may even experience a reprieve for a few days, or a month. But then they are right back at it again, and they come to doubt the Bible or their own sincerity.

> *Victory over a besetting sin is normally a process, not a moment's event.*

Victory will begin to be realized when we tell God in clear terms that we want to surrender our sin to him. We do not have permission to put God off a second longer. But victory over a besetting sin is normally a process, not a moment's event. And it is entirely within the parameters of God's plan that you will face temptations and learn to say no to them.

> For the grace of God that brings salvation has appeared to all men. It *teaches* us to say "No" to ungodliness [whatever goes against the Living God] and worldly passions [cravings], and to live self-controlled, upright and godly lives in this present age.[10]

"Teaching" doesn't take place in a moment; it clearly involves an ongoing work of grace. Let's build on this, and consider what Paul says about surrender:

> Just as you used to offer the parts of your body in slavery to impurity and to ever-increasing wickedness, so now offer them in slavery to righteousness, leading to holiness.[11]

When you were a baby, did you decide, "I'm going to be very wicked"? No! You made a lot of decisions, some major and some trivial, which led you downward by fits and starts. Even so, the new way of living is a series of decisions.
Paul returns to that theme later in Romans:

> Therefore, I urge you, brothers, in view of God 's mercy, to offer your bodies as living sacrifices, holy and pleasing to God—which is your spiritual worship.[12]

Now, I have been told in a dozen sermons that in the Greek, "offer" *really* means "offer once and for all, in a point of time." In fact, that is not what it says, as any of my first-year Greek students could tell you. In the Greek as in the English, Paul is simply saying "offer your bodies."
Notice, however, that Paul uses the language of the Old Testament system of animal sacrifices: He wants living peo-

ple to give themselves over to God just as wholly as a sac-
rificial animal was given over.

How often did the Jews bring sacrifices? Once in a lifetime? In rare moments of spiritual commitment? At special
retreats or seminars? No! They brought them regularly! We
too must offer ourselves to God fully and decisively, yet on
a regular basis.

Of course, we would all prefer a once-and-for-all solution to addiction. We sigh, "Why can't I put my awful problem on the altar, clamp it down, and lock in victory? I've
shown some willingness, so why does God refuse to answer
my prayer to take it away from me?"

The problem is this: that while I'd like to sign myself over
to righteousness for the rest of my life, my resolve is too
weak. How can I tell God "never again" and keep a straight
face when I know how wishy-washy I can be toward my
own sinful cravings?

Remember, too, that God's goal is that you be dependent
upon him. Be grateful that those nagging temptations toward addiction can be defeated and the whole experience
can be rolled over into a closer walk with him.

Surrendering to God is much more difficult than check-
ing yourself into a treatment program or deciding to attend
a meeting, as even A. A. literature underscores. Joan called
a local minister two or three times to get him to come over
and get Ron straightened out, but what could he do? Nei-
ther your pastor nor counselor can bend your will to serve
God; there is no magic pill to swallow or formula to repeat
(or book to read!). Rather, the summons to the addict is
clear: gather up your whole mind, will, body, and surrender and keep surrendering all to God.

"Surrender" is a good religious word; but what, you ask,
is a surrendered life supposed to look like? Does it mean
that if you put forth any effort at all, you're just getting in
God's way?

It's hard to see any command to "go all limp" in Romans 6, and Paul himself will later share that his life involves "struggling with all [Christ's] energy, which so powerfully works in me."[13] It is not lived by God alone (you step aside and do nothing), nor by the Christian alone (you drive yourself to live up to the gospel). The Christian life is lived by the Christian with God's power. Ask yourself whether that fits you. Are you consistently turning to God for help when temptation arises? Do you ever think "I don't need special help, it's just a little temptation"? Are you in fact resisting temptation? If a stronger temptation arose, would the power you have now be sufficient?

As an addict, you need to talk seriously and truthfully with God about your problem, and pray in specifics. Carl says something like this:

> Father, I confess to you that I eat compulsively and that this sin drives me away from your presence. I surrender myself to you today, and specifically I turn this sinful addiction over to you. Grant that I might walk in freedom from food obsession and overeating and glorify you, Lord, as the desire of my heart. I ask this through my King and Savior, the Lord Jesus Christ. Amen.

How often does Carl do this? As often as he needs to! He will certainly want to nip it in the bud by speaking with God even before he faces his breakfast. He also needs to turn it over to God whenever he feels temptation of any sort.

True prayer is not an abracadabra, and it may not be long before Carl struggles with these thoughts. Am I really willing to leave the kingdom of slaves today? Am I lying even to myself? Might Carl's prayer be short-circuited by the quiet thought that he can always sneak a cupcake . . . and later confess it, of course?

God is fully aware of how much unwillingness still lies within you, but he still calls you to immediate surrender.

Come near to God and he will come near to you. Wash your hands, you sinners, and purify your hearts, you double-minded.[14]

If you are struggling with some nonessential substance or activity (alcohol, cocaine, tobacco), you will undoubtedly need to refrain totally from it as a way of life. While it might be argued that Christ can give you the power, for example, to drink wine with your meals, what would be the point of trying?

For those who, like Carl, are consumed with one of life's necessities (sleep, exercise, work), the problem of abstinence is trickier: you can live without cocaine but not without food! Carl will need to define what constitutes compulsive eating or overeating, and then develop some sort of food plan. It is crucial that he not view his program as a diet; he is not trying to lose weight, but to define the boundaries that will help him stay free from his addiction. His prayer is that he might live within those boundaries.

Today, in Christ, in God's power, in real surrender . . . you, too, can learn to just say "No."

Outline Summary

We've covered a lot of ground in this chapter. Let's stop and summarize what you must know, whom you must trust, and how you must act if you are to break free of the kingdom of slaves.

Knowing
- know that the Living God is God alone, and all-powerful
- know that you are designed to worship, and had best worship the Living God

- know that the Fall has twisted and perverted all your faculties, and that only God can save you for himself

Trusting
- trust Christ to recover you once and for all from the real power of the Kingdom of Slavery (conversion)
- trust that all power resides in Christ, and that he will deliver you from addiction if he so pleases

Acting
- consciously, truthfully surrender your life and your addiction to the Living God through Jesus Christ
- live the right way as God works in you with his power

ASSIGNMENTS

1. Compose a prayer of surrender to God. Name the specific problem you have, and confess your complete dependence upon God and his power.

2. Study the New Testament's teaching about "self-control" (Acts 24:25; Gal. 5:22–23; 1 Thess. 5:6; 2 Tim. 1:7; Titus 1:8; 2:11–14; 1 Peter 1:13; 2 Peter 1:5–9). How does that concept apply to Christians? How does self-control relate to the power of the cross?

3. Read Isaiah 44:6–23 and make three lists: (1) how is my addiction like an idol? (2) how is a man-made Higher Power like an idol? (3) how is the true God able to help me?

Introductory quotations: Mark 10:47; Colossians 1:12–14.

4

Counterattacks of the Dark Kingdom

Dangers to Spot

Because of the LORD's great love we are not consumed,
  for his compassions never fail.
They are new every morning;
  great is your faithfulness.
                        —The Lamentations of Jeremiah

  My hope is built on nothing less
      than Jesus' blood and righteousness;
  I dare not trust the sweetest frame,
      but wholly lean on Jesus' name.
  On Christ, the solid rock I stand:
  All other ground is sinking sand.
                        —"The Solid Rock,"
                            by Edward Mote

It's a quiet Friday evening in late summer . . .

  "My name is Ron, and I am a grateful recovering alcoholic." "Hi, Ron!" "Hi, everyone. As of this past Friday, it's been six months since my last drink."

Across town, Sue is going shopping for the first time in weeks; she wants to pick out some school clothes for the kids. On this trip she checks through the list of what she really needs as her husband Carl hunts for a parking space. Sue suddenly looks up and says, "It's best for me if we don't go in the entrance by the department store." Carl grunts his assent and swings around to the other side. Later on in the mall they run into Sue's friend Jackie by the shoe store. "Carl, my goodness, I almost didn't recognize you!" she exclaims. "Just exactly how much weight have you lost?"

These three are in the business of living without their addictions, just this one day in late summer. And in church this past Sunday, Carl and Sue met that new believer, Ron, with his still-doubting wife Joan; together they rose to sing about God's kingdom.

> All hail the power of Jesus' name!
> Let angels prostrate fall.
> Bring forth the royal diadem
> And crown him Lord of all!

How wonderful they feel! And if this seems good, remember—the universe is not focused on how we human beings are feeling, but on God. You can imagine how this looks to him. He now enjoys a special relationship with these reconciled people. He loves them, and is loved in return; from his viewpoint, it is very good.

So the battle is over and the good guys won, right?

Not exactly.

Addiction will not let you go so easily. Just as Pharaoh sent his chariots after the escaping Israelites, so the dark kingdom will throw weapons at your fleeing form. For the rest of their lives our friends can expect to feel the tug from their old ways. We all love what is familiar, and although their experiences were ugly, they were as comfortable as an old pair of loafers.

Fresh dangers are on the horizon.

Danger #1: Not Attending to Life in the Present

One of the best pieces of wisdom to come out of the Twelve-Step movement is the slogan "Just For Today," meaning that sobriety must be lived one day at a time. They in turn distilled it from passages such as this:

> Therefore do not worry about tomorrow, for tomorrow will worry about itself. Each day has enough trouble of its own.[1]

Did you ever notice that addicts cannot seem to focus on what they are doing today? Some brood over the past, on those people who have done them wrong, on the mistakes they have made. They end up bitter and unable to cope with the life they have today. They reach for their substance to ease the misery. Or they pour their energy into an imaginary future. Sue wrestles with anxiety: what if Carl gets fired? What if they lose the house? Other days, she relies on the fantasy of a future when things will be perfect: oh, yes, her life will be well-organized and she will find happiness . . . "some day." Of course, that day will never come, and Sue's mental confusion can leave her immobilized.

"To-morrow, and to-morrow, and to-morrow" said Shakespeare's MacBeth, and so too the addict. Tomorrow the diet! Tomorrow I'll start spending less, and saving more! I'll cut down, starting tomorrow . . . or, no, starting the first of the month . . . or as a New Year's resolution. But tomorrow never seems to arrive, and today is drained of vitality. The solution? A dear friend likes to say: I can dream about playing the piano "some day," but what I really need to do is take a piano lesson today.

God did not design Adam and Eve to stew over the past or to fret about the future: "Hey, Eve, remember that tangerine we had last Thursday? You know, now I'm thinking that we should've eaten half and saved half; we'll never see the likes of that one again!" How absurd! How can they live either in the past or the future when God may be loved and enjoyed *today?*

Ron should not spend his summer brooding over whether he'll take a drink over Labor Day weekend. His best defense against a future slip is to walk with the Living God in sobriety in the present hour.

It takes concentration not to skid away from our true focus, that of living for God today.

🕇 The end of all things is near. Therefore be clear minded and self-controlled so that you can pray.[2]

Why does this come with such difficulty? Could it be that we secretly want to play God? Do we harbor the fantasy that if we concentrate hard enough, we can change the future or alter the past? Perhaps Jesus was reminding us that we are not divine, but creatures, when he said, "Who of you by worrying can add a single hour to his life?"[3]

That truth can protect your wallet as well as your soul. For example, a multibillion dollar diet industry is twisting Carl's arm to "lose weight fast." Smokers too are vulnerable to "fast," "easy" gimmicks. Don't ever feel pressured by some manmade schedule!

🕇 Danger #2: Underestimating the Power of Evil

Christians can easily become blasé about evil. Ron may live for a few years without alcohol, and the memories of the hellish experiences will start to fade. Will he become sedated into thinking that things will go along just like they are now?

One of the most frequent commands in the New Testament is the byword "Be watchful!" Even as they depend upon God's power, Christians are to beware of temptations. Peter even goes into the details.

> All of you, clothe yourselves with humility toward one another, because, "God opposes the proud but gives grace to the humble." Humble yourselves, therefore, under God's mighty hand, that he may lift you up in due time. Cast all your anxiety on him because he cares for you. Be self-controlled and alert. Your enemy the devil prowls around like a roaring lion looking for someone to devour. Resist him, standing firm in the faith.[4]

Many churches are casting the devil out of their doctrine, usually because they don't want to appear superstitious. But evil is not just some philosophical category; it is persistent because there is a powerful intelligence behind it. Small wonder that many addicts come to believe in the devil's existence.

When does evil play tricks on your mind?

When It Feeds You the Myth of Invulnerability

Have you ever heard a speech like this? "Why I deliberately walk right down Oak Street, right past all those prostitutes and massage parlors, and it doesn't bother me a bit! God has given me the power to resist, so why should I let it be a problem?"

God is piously invoked, but what this brother is really impressed with is his own abilities. If he's not careful, he may get the wind knocked right out of him. In an addict, that old pattern of "terminal uniqueness" ("I'm not like all the others") may resurface, decked out with references to God.

Don't misunderstand me! I believe that God protects me from harm: still, I wear my seat belt; I never stand up in a small boat; I do not eat meat that's been sitting out on the counter all day. Otherwise I would be presumptuous of God, pushing to find the limits. The Bible calls this the sin of "testing God." It is the exact temptation that Jesus faced when the devil took him to a high place of the Temple, and told him to throw himself down: after all, didn't the Bible say that God's angels would watch over him? Jesus responded, "It says: 'Do not put the Lord your God to the test.'"[5]

Some preachers give the tempter a head start: "God doesn't grant partial victory!" they proclaim. "If this sobriety is from God, then it's bound to be permanent!" This attitude is sometimes called "triumphalism."

But when did God write you a guarantee that you will triumph always? He will allow you to turn over addiction to him, but he will not take away your ability to rebel. This is why he tells us, "come near to God, and he will come near to you."[6]

When It Fools You into Setting Your Own Trap

Addicts may be oblivious to dangers that are perfectly obvious to everyone else. If there is any doubt, it's best to act decisively. That's why Carl asked Sue if they could keep the cupboards free of potato chips—he doesn't want to run into his old buddies some evening.

All of us need to perform a ruthless housecleaning of our lives. What are the sights, sounds, or smells of your addiction? Ron will want to rid his entire home of bottles. He needs to stay clear of his drinking buddies. He even needs to trash the hat he always wore while drinking in front of the ball game on TV. As one book puts it

Most relapses to a person's primary addiction are preceded by use of other mood-changers that have been previously associated with your primary drug. For example, cocaine addicts whose cocaine use had been associated with seeing prostitutes find that even thoughts and fantasies about these sexual encounters will elicit strong cravings for cocaine (Washton and Boundy 1989, 161).

<u>Appreciate your own weaknesses and take it easy on</u> <u>yourself. Yes, resisting temptation may make you a stronger</u> <u>person, but it is best to root out every single unnecessary</u> <u>risk. "Do not give the devil a foothold."[7]</u>

What is your weakness? Traveling alone seems to trouble most addicts—does it affect you that way? Do you know what sets your addiction in motion? A sweeping "depression brings it on" may not be sharp enough. What sort of depression? What seems to cause this type of depression? Do you also think of picking it up when you are, say, exhilarated?

When It Tells You "Just This Once"

If it's not subtle, it's not temptation! That's why "just once won't hurt" is such an effective line. All around are people who can drink a beer, or go on a shopping spree, or take a sleeping pill, and it's not fair. It doesn't hurt them, so why should it hurt you?

Another crafty lie is this one: "Hey, even if you fall into sin, it will make you that much stronger, because you'll remember how awful it was!" But keep in mind that addiction is a life-dominating habit. Just one barbiturate can trigger a whole web of reactions; that old good feeling will come flooding back, and that will be followed by a whispered, "just a second time won't hurt."

K Danger #3: Intimacy and Detaching

You can spot the addict on the committee, running things, criticizing, controlling the situation . . . or sitting quietly in the background, offering little, maybe even sulking. For many addicts, to be just one of a group is to be "one of the herd."

But God commands us to be contributing members of groups—with the family, at the workplace, in church—without living the fantasy of being the group's savior. <u>The goal of each Christian is straightforward: to demonstrate godly love to others.</u>

It is impossible for us to love too much, if by love we mean doing for another person the good that we would do for ourselves. But in choosing to love, we will want to avoid these two extremes:

- making our loved ones over into our own ideal of what they should be. We should encourage others on to Christ-likeness, not to Me-likeness.
- thinking of ourselves to the exclusion of others. Addicts have many needs, and to some, selfishness is a virtue: "After all I've tried to do for other people, now I just need to focus on being kind to me." Are you really no longer responsible to love?

Here's another problem area: long experience has led A. A. to discourage "Thirteenth Stepping," that is, taking a member of the opposite sex as a sponsor or close confidant. Spirituality and sexuality are very closely related, both being rooted in our personhood. Regular sharing with a person of the opposite sex often leads to physical and emotional intimacy. Never presume that you've outgrown this one! The loving thing to do is to avoid bringing trouble on both parties.

> You, my brothers, were called to be free. But do not use your freedom to indulge the sinful nature; rather, serve one another in love.[8]

Danger #4: Paralyzing Guilt

Liz has abstained from workaholism for months now. But one week she starts staying at the office for twelve hours at a time. Her family, God, church, the whole process known as living all vanish as she gets her "high." Even that nagging feeling of guilt doesn't slow her down. In fact, the worse she feels, the more she takes refuge in her drug of choice.

Guilt may drive you to repentance, but it is also a strong weapon in the armory of the evil kingdom. When Carl used to feel depressed over his hefty appearance, he'd cheer himself up with an ice cream sundae.

Our society has bought into the myth that "it's bad to feel guilty," and it urges us to label those feelings as "false guilt." But addicts who know the Living God accept that when they practice their addiction, they will FEEL guilty, because in fact they ARE guilty. The feeling of guilt—like hunger, thirst, pain—is a signal that something is amiss.

Don't try to blot out guilt; rather, turn to God who is "faithful and just and will forgive us our sins and purify us from all unrighteousness."[9] And once we have gotten the matter straight with God and with people we have harmed, we have then gained the right to dismiss that guilty feeling.

The addicts' main risk is getting stranded in the middle of the road: not feeling bad enough to ask for God's pardon, nor good enough to live joyfully. A clean break with sin before the Living God is the answer to life in that twilight zone.

Danger #5: Boredom

Addicts cannot seem to sit still. They fidget, they get up and pace the floor, they look like kids trapped inside on a rainy day.

Such boredom has its own perils. In the past, it signalled that it was time to spice things up with your drug of choice. Even today, you may fall back into your pattern for no better reason than "there's nothing to do."

Walking with the Lord has a way of putting texture into everyday life. Fill those newly liberated hours, but not with another addiction, not with busyness, not with TV, not even with a church meeting every day, but with LIFE. Learn to "seize the day."

Danger #6: Becoming Addicted to Addiction

Most new members of a recovery group will want to start off with total immersion. Newcomers to A. A. are urged to attend "90 meetings in 90 days." So much needs to be covered, and quickly. Afterward there will be a natural tapering off.

On the other hand, there are people who have gotten "hooked" on recovery meetings. Because they are addicts, they take even recovery to an extreme. They may regard their group as their Higher Power, and so life, God, and fellowship are all rolled up into those special hours. They will attend a meeting four, five, seven nights a week. They suspect that they have other addictions, and try out new meetings. Hour after hour is spent on the phone with their new friends. Their families, which have coped for years with addiction, may be killed by its cure.

God has not made us for recovery—he has made us for life with him. Group meetings are not to be a device for avoiding life.

Danger #7: Trying to Cope without the Living God

It is impossible to stay neutral: either you stand for the Living God or you stand for bondage to the dominion of darkness. "Our hearts find no peace until they rest in you." How contemporary does Augustine's observation sound! Addicts jam one thing after another into their inner void, but peace eludes them. It may be best, when you remove the junk from that God-shaped hole, that you just live with the void until the Living God fills it with his presence.

Of course, if we're right and there is a devil, then it is his job is to keep you from the Living God. It's also to be taken for granted that he wants to keep you hooked on a substance. But if you were the devil, and you had to give up one claim or the other, which would you let drop? I'm pretty sure that he would be satisfied if a drinker got freed from alcohol so long as he believed in no god, or relied on some hazy Higher Power . . . or for that matter, held the true God at arm's length.

One diet club uses the seemingly logical slogan "nothing tastes as good as thin feels." But if you think that compulsive eaters will feel so good being thin and healthy that they will never again want to overeat, you're kidding yourself. They need a "reason for being" higher than mere slimness; they need the Living God.

A Note of Hope: The Battle Is Not Endless

There are days when this process seems to be no more than a mindless cycle of attack and counterattack. Even the monotony of steady victory can become a temptation to grab hold of some other form of excitement.

Keep your final goal in mind. The goal of Twelve-Step recovery programs is that "we will comprehend the word *serenity* and we will know peace" (A. A. World Service 1976, 83–84). The goal of the gospel on the other hand is that we be right with God. When the apostle says "we have peace with God through our Lord Jesus Christ,"[10] he is not stating that we have peaceful feelings (although we do). It means that, objectively, the war between us and God has ceased, and God has called us into his holy kingdom.

The Christian life is a temporary period of testing for those who are escaping from the dark kingdom into the kingdom of God. And so, even in the most exhilarating moments, we are merely getting a glimpse of our goal. In the end, we will finally experience life as God intended. We will never again be tempted by any substance or activity that is a substitute for the Living God. We can pick up where Adam and Eve left off and enjoy a Paradise of meaning, acceptance, and pleasure with our one true king.

Your battle with the dark kingdom today is propelling you toward that hope.

ASSIGNMENTS

1. Make a list of all the ways you have been tempted by your pattern sin. When this is done, carefully read through 1 Corinthians 10:1–13, especially verse 13. How does this passage comment on your experience? Warning: your addiction will not limit itself to the tried and true temptations; this list should grow over time.

2. Read *The Holy War* by John Bunyan. It is available in modern paraphrased versions. You might want to write in the margins how you have experienced the different types of temptation that Bunyan describes.

Introductory quotations: Lamentations 3:22–23.

5

Living at Peace in the Kingdom of God

Getting Back Together

It matters what you do.

It matters what you do, because it matters to God.
If it matters to God, it matters.

When you go astray, when you hurt yourself and others,
it matters, because it matters to God.

When you disobey God repeatedly,
it matters to God
every single time.

Addiction takes otherwise normal people and turns
them into recluses. This is why a part of your task will be

reconciling with other people and with God himself. "Reconciliation" is a good Bible word; when two hostile parties get back together in peace, you have reconciliation. And if anyone has created hostile parties, it is the addict.

Your Life Matters

From Darwin we learn that survival belongs, not to the best behaved, but to the fittest. According to Freud, the conscience is just society's way of reining in our antisocial impulses. And sociologists remind us that our behavior is not right or wrong: it just is.

They all work on the assumption that your life choices ultimately do not matter.

They are wrong.

Your Life Matters to God . . .

I look down at an ant crawling over the floor. Whether that ant turns to the right or left, eats lunch at noon or 1 P.M., lives or dies makes no difference at all to me. And I have to wonder: is this how God views me? Too small to be bothered with, compared with his cosmic plans? The answer is "No." When we say that God is great, we mean that he is able to fathom our innermost thoughts and motives, and that he cares. God regards your actions as right, or wrong, or a mixture of the two; but never is God indifferent.

> O LORD, you have searched me and you know me.
> You know when I sit and when I rise;
>   you perceive my thoughts from afar.
> You discern my going out and my lying down;
>   you are familiar with all my ways.
> Before a word is on my tongue
>   you know it completely, O LORD.[1]

. . . And Your Life Matters to Others

Every Christmas the TV networks haul out the sentimental classic "It's a Wonderful Life." Poor, downtrodden George Bailey has come to doubt his own worth. But he cries out "I want to live!" when he sees how his life has touched others.

Even if you live as a hermit, you have touched others for good or ill, and it matters to them and to God.

Reconciliation with God through Christ

In God's mind, your highest priority is to be reconciled with him through the cross. But people have misgivings. "When I go to God and confess my compulsive violent anger for the tenth time this week, will he really hear me? When do I reach the cutoff point, beyond which he says 'forget it'?"

Several points need to be kept in mind. One, that God's grace is unlimited. Two, that God is very interested in breaking our pattern sins, so that we won't have to keep confessing the same thing. Three, that our confession may be amiss—perhaps we just want to get rid of the guilt we feel, but we don't have any serious desire to change.

We certainly want to reject the heresy of "cheap grace," that we can get as dirty as we like, and occasionally check in with God to get hosed down. God's grace has come at a terrible expense, and he is outraged when it is trampled. But accept that the cross is not there to fix up "nice folks" with the Living God. No; the people God had in mind were running away as hard as they could. So you see, you are not impressing him with your humility when you imagine that your sins are too big for the cross.

Reconciliation with Other People

This may seem a tougher chore than asking God to forgive you, but it will be beneficial for a number of reasons:

you might help your family to come together, and you can
settle your own conscience. But the best motivation is,
again, that it is important to God.

Reconciling with Those You've Harmed

People are still talking about the fireworks at that grad-
uation party last summer over at the Nelson house. A drink
helped one guest, our old friend Ron, to lose his inhibitions.
As the evening wore on he became a real prize: abandon-
ing his wife Joan, he made lewd remarks to the other
women. Next, he drew you into an endless argument, even
though you said you agreed with his point of view; but minutes later he changed his mind and blasted the opinion he
had been defending. His main contribution to the night's
fun was to dash to the powder room, making it almost in
time to vomit, loudly and incessantly. After he took his
leave, you could hear him cursing out whoever it was that
blocked in his car.

Things didn't look much better the morning after. It was
Monday, and he pressured Joan to call the company with
the news that he had "the flu." Joan wasn't having a great
day, either. She heard it from the bill collectors; from the po-
lice officer, who wanted to know if Ron was at his bar the
previous Tuesday; from the Nelsons, who now had a broken
taillight to remember Ron's grand exit. Beyond this, she
caught a litany of complaints from Ron, who blamed her
nagging for his splitting headache and his craving for drink.

Part of Ron's new life must be to make things right with
those he hurt while he was still drinking.

Okay, you say, I grant that drunks and junkies do some
pretty vile things, but what about an addiction that doesn't
hurt anyone? If I overeat, I'm just harming myself, right? The
same is true if I overspend or smoke pot in my own home.

True, many addicts will have to dig around in order to
find out how they've harmed people. But it won't take long

before you have a good list. For example, have you neglected people in favor of your substance? Have you deprived others of your time? Have you stolen, or misused money that should have been spent more wisely? Have you been dishonest (lying, sneaking, minimizing, rationalizing)? Have you nursed anger or resentment? Have you made yourself and your substance the center of the universe? Jesus said

> Therefore, if you are offering your gift at the altar [i.e., worshiping the Living God] and there remember that your brother has something against you, leave your gift there in front of the altar. First go and be reconciled to your brother; then come and offer your gift.[2]

If you make a list of all persons you have harmed with the intent of reconciling with them, you will need to mention co-workers and employers, friends, fellow church-members, and family members. You may find that the people closest to you—especially spouses—have the hardest time of it.

For their part, the family members of the addict need to think through their own problems. Joan, in fact, has a little addiction of her own: a running fantasy, starring herself as a martyr who strives against the odds, outwitting the creditors, protecting her children, and working hard to reform her man. In fact, she married Ron partly so that she could "fix" him. She knows that God is counting on her to hold back chaos.

She may pray for the day when Ron gets straightened out, but what happens then? Her "reason for being" suddenly evaporates.

It is a mistake to "blame the victim," but few people in a troubled family are without fault. Even if Joan's only vice is resentment, she needs to deal with that before God and her husband.

Ron can't solve his wife's problems any more than she could cure his—he needs to focus on his own amends and to remember that simplicity is the key to any good apology. Isn't it lame when an apology is really an accusation in disguise? Ron makes a move in the right direction, but in the end he blows it with Joan.

> Honey, I really messed up last June when I went on that bender over at the Nelsons. Boy, did I need a drink—that was the week you were all over me about the electricity being cut off, and . . .

Off the two of them go on a long argument about who was to blame and in what proportion. How much better it would have been for Ron merely to focus on his own fault, and then move on. Otherwise, his tendency to justify himself may drive him, quite literally, to drink. His repentance would be so much sweeter if he could bring himself to say

> Joan, I want to apologize for the way I acted at the Nelson's last summer. I know now that I can 't handle any alcohol; but I drank that night, and ended up hurting you and driving our friends away. Will you forgive me?

Period. He should be contrite and look it, and he can talk further if Joan needs it, but for now that is all he has to say. He doesn't need to fish around for a counterapology from Joan, who in fact *did* nag him all that week. And when he stops playing games, Joan may find it easier to face her own faults.

He also needs to think in terms of real restitution. The Old Testament gives clear guidelines for how it was to be done (note how Zacchaeus follows them in Luke 19:8), and the New Testament echoes the spirit of those laws.

He who has been stealing must steal no longer, but must work, doing something useful with his own hands, that he may have something to share with those in need.[3]

When we restore what we have taken, we must do so humbly, simply, and reliably. Most people would rather write off a debt than listen to a string of vague promises.

Lastly, Ron needs to see the difference between restitution and smothering: "I've got to make it up to the kids for the years I cheated them of support, guidance, my attendance at their ball games. From now on I'm going to attend to them every waking minute!" Slavish devotion is not good for anyone. The best gift you can give to your former victims is yourself, free from addiction, and reclaiming your humanity in Christ.

Living with the Open Wound

On a different level, it will help if Ron appreciates that people are not waiting around to forgive him. Part of his problem is that he has gone on the wagon before, and he even spilled a few tears whenever things got too tight. When Ron truly tries to reconcile, he may encounter anger, disbelief, and rejection.

Ron's old reaction would be typical for an addict: "Look, if you can stand there with your holier-than-thou attitude and not even accept a sincere attempt at reconciliation, then forget you!" Today Ron needs to accept that he has helped to create that distrust as part of the price of his drinking.

When you go about to make amends, you may be surprised at the amount of goodwill you encounter. However, you may run into individuals who refuse to give you their forgiveness for one reason or another. There are several versions:

- They refuse to forgive: whether they are sullen or violent or coldly polite, these people will not accept your apology.

- They forgive but don't forget: they mouth the right words, but act as if nothing has changed.
- They laugh it off: in a time when the concept of personal responsibility has taken a beating, people are uncomfortable with repentance. And so you will hear, "Oh, forget it!" or "Don't worry about it, nobody's perfect." For some, this is just their way of saying that they forgive you without making a fuss. It may help if you press them just a bit to say those words—not only will you feel better, but in speaking it aloud, they may feel that the situation truly is resolved. But for others, this is their way of saying "No."

What if a person ultimately refuses to reconcile with you? Accept that situation with grace. Remember that, after years of hurting this person, you have come out of the blue with the announcement that you are setting things right. They may need to watch you for a while to see if you are genuine. You may want to give it a second try, but after that it is best to leave the situation open-ended: "Well, Frank, I see that you don't feel like forgiving me today, but I want you to know that I'm always open to straightening things out. I hope we can set things right at some point."

Reconciling with Those Who Have Harmed You

The Twelve Steps focus on making amends with people the addict has harmed, to the neglect of seeking reconciliation with those who have harmed us. To their credit, they are following a strong line of reasoning: addicts typically feel that they are the world's victims. For them to go around asking people for apologies is dangerous, but it is clearly God's will.

If your brother sins against you, go and show him his fault, just between the two of you. If he listens to you, you have won your brother over.[4]

Needless to say, this mission will require patience, tact, and above all, humility. You will find help if you go over your plan of action with a godly friend and ask for candid feedback.

Reconciliation with the Church

You may figure that you can grow in Christ just as well without the frustration of other people. Besides, church doesn't "do it" for you, not when you can spend your social time with other recovering addicts.

But it will please God—and help your fellow Christians—if you will swallow your pride and submit to being an ordinary sheep in an ordinary flock.

> And let us consider how we may spur one another on toward love and good deeds. Let us not give up meeting together, as some are in the habit of doing, but let us encourage one another—and all the more as you see the Day approaching.[5]

You need help to grow closer to the Living God, and God tells you that church is essential for growth. To spurn the church is to spurn God's wise plan for you. In short, you'd be thinking like an addict.

The Problem of Rejection

Maybe you are a church member, or perhaps you've left off going to church. Either way, those church folks look like they're just waiting to pin the "sinner" label on you.

I suspect that a lot of that is in your mind, but let's go with the thought: yes, some churches have a hard time accepting the person who is fighting a sin habit. Have you ever gone to an amusement park and taken a look at some of the rides? In front of them will stand a cutout of a smiling clown with a message: "You must be *this* tall to ride the Whippersnapper." Well, a few churches do give the impression that "you need to be THIS righteous to come in!" And if you really wanted to, you could sniff out some two-facedness: the welcome mat is out for the bigoted and the gossip, but not for the cocaine or sex addict. The preacher condemns the self-indulgence of alcohol abuse just before devouring a whole chicken at the church dinner. And most Christians can't have a Bible study without gallons of coffee to perk them up.

Yes, yes, *YES*, all true, but remember: Their mistake does not lie in calling you a sinner. You are, in fact, a sinner, and probably a fine example of one. Their error is that they sometimes forget that they are sinners too.

Finding the Right Church

You may find yourself looking around for a new church to join. What should you be looking for?

Don't be taken in by surface appearances: there are shallow churches that feature wall-to-wall excitement, and there are vital churches that come off a bit drab. What you need is a church that does well in three crucial areas.

1. Is the Church in Love with God's Word, the Bible?
   Does it believe God's Word, through and through? Are the sermons and lessons driven by the Bible, or do they just include a verse or two for show? Does it urge you to read the Bible on your own? Do you feel motivated to learn more?
2. Is the Church Centered in the Cross?
   The cross shows us God's disgust toward sin, but his love for the offender. A cross-centered church speaks

out against sin in all its forms. It also emphasizes the depths of God's mercy.

3. Is the Church a Place of True Fellowship? Do your conversations go beyond sports and the weather to the things of God? Do people volunteer what God is doing in their lives lately? Do you feel yourself being challenged and growing as a Christian through knowing them?

If you think you might have trouble discerning these things, get some advice from another mature Christian, one who respects these three priorities.

Working in the Church—Superstar or Servant?

A man or woman with a past can give a testimony that sounds glamorous and dangerous. Who can electrify the youth group if not the "former drug addict and cop-killer who found Christ"?

But a church that idolizes you may end up destroying you. You must know deep down that your only reason for being is to glorify God. After all . . .

who makes you different from anyone else? What do you have that you did not receive? And if you did receive it, why do you boast as though you did not?[6]

You don't need to share all your personal details with everyone, but you must make very certain that you speak only the truth. Do you leave out certain key facts about your past life? Do you blame others when that is not quite accurate? Or do you glorify your past to give yourself the glow of notoriety? Speaking the truth means telling the facts as they are, without embellishment.

Once you find a solid church, concentrate on serving it in love and humility. One ministry may be to start a support group for other addicts, such as a chapter of Overcomers Outreach. But remember—you are a casualty yourself, not some expert at fixing others' lives!

> Finally, all of you, live in harmony with one another; be sympathetic, love as brothers, be compassionate and humble.[7]

By all means, allow the church time to observe your life and to put you even in humble positions of service. No kidding, there is no better medicine than mopping the floor or helping out in the nursery. These experiences will remind you of God's grace and of the importance of being a part of his people.

ASSIGNMENTS

1. Make a list of your offenses against God, noting those which you have not yet gotten right with him. Speak to God about each of them in particular. Let the peace and forgiveness of Christ replace the darkness and confusion of your guilt.

2. Practice speaking the truth. Think of some experience you have had in the last day or so. It doesn't have to be spiritual, just something you can remember and describe. Recall it for someone else, telling him or her exactly what happened. Do so without exaggeration one way or another. Try it with another event tomorrow, and continue to practice truth-telling until it becomes second nature.

6

Ongoing Life
in the Kingdom of God

Recovery Tools

> In the future, when your son asks you, "What is the meaning of the stipulations, decrees and laws the LORD our God has commanded you?" tell him: "We were slaves of Pharaoh in Egypt, but the LORD brought us out of Egypt with a mighty hand."
>
> —The Book of Deuteronomy

Recovery, like life, is a process of daily growth. Ron will spend months and years establishing new patterns, learning how to deal with life without a chemical escape. Any recovery group will have a list of activities that will reinforce your first few steps in the right direction. Overeaters

Anonymous even publishes a pamphlet called "Tools of Recovery," the tools being Abstinence, Sponsorship, Meetings, Telephone, Writing, Literature, Anonymity, and Service.

How effective are the traditional recovery tools for the Christian? We'll look specifically at the value of support groups, mentors, service, and spiritual growth.

Support Groups

A recovery support group is composed of people who have had a common addiction, and who now gather for mutual help. Twelve-Step groups have been multiplying at an astonishing rate. A. A. alone went from 28,000 groups worldwide in 1976 to 94,000 in 1992, with a membership now topping 2 million. Today you can even attend electronic meetings via home computer! And as soon as A. A. began to log some success, other Twelve-Step fellowships were founded, starting with Al-Anon for family members of alcoholics. These various groups have mushroomed across the globe (White and Madara 1992).

   1935 Alcoholics Anonymous (94,000 groups)
   1951 Al-Anon (32,000 groups)
   1953 Narcotics Anonymous (22,000 groups)
   1957 Gamblers Anonymous (1200 groups)
   1960 Overeaters Anonymous (9968 groups)

From these groups have sprung hundreds of new organizations, such as Emotions Anonymous, Debtors Anonymous, and Sex and Love Addicts Anonymous (see Appendix A). You have only to match your problem with the appropriate outfit and then find the meeting nearest you. If you have gone through a rehab program, typically you will be pointed toward a Twelve-Step group for your follow-up.

Almost everyone involved in the Twelve Steps will be keenly in favor of your going. For some of these people, the Steps are the only way, and any suggestion to the contrary is heresy. In the evangelical mainstream today there is a growing acceptance of Twelve-Step meetings at least as a supplement to the church's ministry.

Opposition comes from many quarters. Despite the churches' description of A. A. as a "secular Twelve-Step program," the group is spiritual and pluralistic. Statistics are hard to come by, but thousands, perhaps millions of drunks avoid A. A. because it is "religious."

But many churches will oppose A. A., too. Some will argue that A. A. constitutes an alternative religious system, in which a Christian has no business being. Then, too, many Christians have been put off when they encountered nebulous concepts of the Higher Power, psychobabble, New Age terms, vulgar language, or smoking. You may get an opinion on the matter from your counselor or pastor, but be ready to ask them the reasons WHY they say "yes" or "no" to group meetings.

It probably goes without saying that a Twelve-Step group is not essential to victory, since people kicked their habits for millennia prior to 1935. But should the idea be dismissed altogether? Whether or not Christians should go to A. A. is, of course, God's decision. The Bible, however, does not give specific instructions on this question. And so, you should consider carefully the reasons for and against attending a Twelve-Step meeting. We'll use Alcoholics Anonymous as an example.

Reasons *for* Going:

- Ease of Entry: there are no entry requirements or dues. You may go as often or as seldom as you like.
- A Ready Welcome: A. A. is run by alcoholics, for alcoholics. They are not easily shocked.

- Worldwide Availability: A. A. will always be there, in every city in this country and around the globe.

- Sponsors: Part of the service that an alcoholic is to render to the group is to serve as a mentor to other members. If you lose one sponsor, you can always find another.

- Instant Contact: You can get in touch with other group members through the telephone and meetings.

- Simple, but not Simplistic. "Keep it simple" was a favorite slogan of A. A.'s co-founder, Dr. Bob. The program is designed to be easily remembered and applied.

- Anonymity. It is comforting to be in a meeting where you are known by your first name only. You can share your story, and almost always it will go no further.

Reasons *against* Going:

- Pluralistic Theology of God. You can share about God in general, and you can publicly name Jesus Christ as your Higher Power. Plus, you can share Christ on an individual level. You will be discouraged, however, from dwelling on your distinctively Christian testimony in the meeting. You will also have to put up with hearing all sorts of theologies without complaint.

- Weak Theology of Sin and Redemption. The focus is on the "disease" of alcoholism. Although alcoholics are told to take responsibility for their actions, the idea that they have offended a holy God may be absent. If you are receiving Christian counseling, the two of you will want to walk through the differences between A. A. and the gospel.

- Negative Attitude toward the Church. Since A. A. may be totally accepting of the alcoholic, it may seem a safer haven than the church and more "Christian" in its love.

- Non-Christian Sponsors. They may not have a biblical perspective; or they may be dictatorial and controlling.
- Hypocrisy. A. A.'s do not always live up to their own standards, although this should not seem strange to people who attend a church! Human failings of every sort are in evidence. Meetings for sex addicts in particular have to keep a close lookout for the predations of "wolves."

To almost all Christians who ask me whether they should to go to a Twelve-Step group, my answer is "yes." The benefits will outweigh the disadvantages . . .

if they hold firm to the gospel,

if they do not let A. A. take the place of the church,

if they are able to represent themselves as Christians, and

if they consistently evaluate what they hear by the Bible.

What's it like to go to a Twelve-Step meeting? That's a bit like asking what it's like to go to church—it all depends on which one you go to. In A. A. middle-aged men predominate, while women in their thirties form the biggest bloc within Overeaters Anonymous. Many people are members of more than one group.

A meeting could be a dozen people around a table or a hundred in a large hall. You get more chances to share in a small group, but you can be inconspicuous in a large one! You will be approached with a smile and perhaps the offer of a hug. Introductions are by first name only.

When the meeting begins, there may be a call for newcomers to introduce themselves. Beyond that, most groups will let you sit quietly and listen if that is what you want. The meeting may run from one to two hours. You will hear a mixture of readings from their literature, people telling their stories, and sharing on a chosen topic. As in any group, they will have their own jargon that you will be able to grasp in a meeting or two. They may rise to join in the Serenity Prayer or the Lord's Prayer.

People are not supposed to give advice during a meeting, although they may do so afterward. Nor is anyone allowed to talk out of turn, take part in a dialogue ("cross talk"), or comment on what others have shared.

This is the way it usually works. Gossip is strictly banned but not unheard of, and you may have to sit through an excruciatingly detailed "drunkalogue." But if you will remember that these people are your fellow human beings, flawed like yourself, you should find the meeting a positive, uplifting experience. Concentrating on the Living God, you will be exhorted to draw near to him and surrender yourself to his will.

Some A. A. groups are more Christian than others, but there are no officially Christian chapters of A. A. or the other pluralistic groups. There is however a growing number of recovery groups designed specifically by evangelicals. Alcoholics Victorious has been around since the 1940s; Substance Abusers Victorious and Overeaters Victorious are other Christian groups. The most prominent Christian organization is the fast-growing Overcomers Outreach. O. O. is intended to supplement the pluralistic groups. Thus, a man with a history of drug abuse would go to Narcotics Anonymous for help with his specific substance, and then to Overcomers for Christian input. O. O. meetings are structured the same as other Twelve-Step gatherings, and they include an informal Bible study, personal sharing, and prayer. The Christian fellowship is strengthened by the members' common experience with addiction.

What you should guard against is the danger that with the growing variety of programs, you flit from one to another, looking for the perfect solution and never settling down to doing one thing well. Unfortunately, this trait seems to characterize addicts as a group.

Mentors

Think of other character traits that attend addiction—isolation, self-deception, aimlessness, procrastination, under- or over-confidence—and you will understand why the addict should not attempt to go it alone. Indeed, throughout most of church history, it has been taken for granted that every Christian should seek out a spiritual guide.

In Twelve-Step groups all members, regardless of their longevity in the program, are encouraged to have sponsors. A sponsor is simply a person who is living the steps and who offers you his or her experience, strength, and hope. Personal style will of course vary. If you are in a Twelve-Step group, try to find a sponsor with a firm commitment to Christ.

Must those who guide addicts be former addicts themselves? No, although it helps. But the qualities of a good Christian mentor are the same as those of a solid church in chapter five—in love with God's word, centered in the cross, and able to relate to you about spiritual things.

Without exception, you will want a mentor with whom you will be honest. Resolve that you will tell them when you have had a slip, when you are tempted, and what is tempting to you. For their part, sponsors need to be willing to listen without flinching, and to offer the presence of Christ to you.

Service to Others

Christians sometimes make the error of just taking in; if they feel that they are not growing fast enough, they become voracious, constantly demanding more nourishment. But you will find that the best growth comes with replacing some of your taking with giving.

Paul made a striking statement about giving help to others.

> Brothers, if someone is caught in a sin, you who are spiritual should restore him gently. But watch yourself, or you

also may be tempted. Carry each other's burdens, and in this way you will fulfill the law of Christ. If anyone thinks he is something when he is nothing, he deceives himself. Each one should test his own actions. Then he can take pride in himself, without comparing himself to somebody else, for each one should carry his own load.[1]

Just look at all the lessons for us:

1. We should recognize sin for what it is.
2. Sin can "catch" people in its clutches.
3. Don't try to restore others when you yourself are stumbling.
4. A gentle spirit is a must. God does not call us to scare sinners out of their transgressions by rough treatment.
5. Temptation is to be expected—perhaps our guard is down, or we are not paying attention to our own weaknesses.
6. We can and should help others with their unusual problems ("burdens") while insisting that they be responsible for their own lives before God ("for each one should carry his own load").
7. Christ commands us to love each other, and this is one way in which we might express that love.

Ron, Carl, and Sue will want to avoid two extremes: the extreme of playing Mr. or Ms. Fix-It for everyone's problems; the opposite extreme of begging off, because they have enough troubles of their own.

Spiritual Growth

There is a rising interest in spirituality quite apart from any system of doctrine. Just keep in mind that spirituality and Christianity are not the same thing. An LSD user may be having all sorts of spiritual experiences—"seeing God," hearing voices—but be no closer to the Living God through Jesus Christ.

When we urge you to grow spiritually, we are saying that you need to deepen your surrender to the Living God. Learn to lean on him, or otherwise you will just trade one dependency for another: eating for smoking, gambling for drinking, compulsive anger for drug abuse. The way of freedom from all crutches is open only to redeemed people in the power of the Spirit.

> Therefore do not be foolish, but understand what the Lord's will is. Do not get drunk on wine, which leads to debauchery. Instead, be filled with the Spirit.[2]

Every Christian should be learning what God's will is through a regular and careful study of the Bible, starting with the New Testament, in a readable translation such as the New International Version. Every Christian must be regularly turning to God in order to worship, to confess his or her failures, and to ask for direction.

Let's stay away from a checklist mentality, such as "If you just read the Bible, then things will automatically fall into place." I can't tell you how many seminarians, full-time students of the Bible, fall into pattern sins of one thing or another. Not even a good morning devotional will ward off all evil. I think of those old horror movies, where Dracula is held at bay with a crucifix. I can't remember—did it have to be silver? Or maybe it wasn't a cross, but garlic . . . No matter! In the end, the decisive issues are surrender and obedience, for which there are no substitutes.

Conclusion: Christians Who Walk with a Limp

We have come to the end of our study, and yet it seems like we have only begun to grapple with the realities of the

Living God! But there is just enough room for one more truth; I leave it for you to ponder in your darker hours.

It is just this: You have been through an experience in idolatry and sin that by rights should have destroyed you. Your life was a pattern of making a bad situation worse. Maybe you're lucky even to be alive today. But despite all of this, God has moved with power and liberated you: he struck off your chains and recovered you from the kingdom of bondage.

In the end, it all comes down to God's good grace.

> All of us also lived among [the disobedient] at one time, gratifying the cravings of our sinful nature and following its desires and thoughts. Like the rest, we were by nature objects of wrath.
>
> But because of his great love for us, God, who is rich in mercy, made us alive with Christ even when we were dead in transgressions—it is by grace you have been saved.[3]

I'm going to guess that there will be days when you are tired of walking in your own shoes. Your past catches up to you with vivid reminders of the abuse you once dealt yourself. Having to dodge those same temptations, every day, is getting you down. You look at other Christians who seem to spring along without a care, and you wonder "why me?"

Paul once described how he lived with aggravation of a somewhat different nature. Because of the amount of revelation that was entrusted to him, including a vision of heaven, God allowed him to be beset by a "thorn in his flesh." Whether a physical ailment or something else, this annoying and painful affliction bothered Paul, as far as we know, until he died. But he could cope, because one day the Living God spoke directly to him and said: "My grace is sufficient for you, for my power is made perfect in weakness."[4]

This applies to you, with some qualifications: for example, God did not saddle you with the burden of addiction.

He did not lead you into temptation. He did not make you take the first dose, then the second. He did not teach you to become so dependent on a thing that your whole life was ordered by it.

BUT . . . he did rescue you from that and more through Christ. And because of that evil experience, you will be even more aware of the truth, "My grace is sufficient for you." It's not every Christian who can know so immediately and deeply how much he or she really depends on God just to get through the day. But like the apostle, you can be sure that the grace of the Living God is sufficient—*easily* sufficient!—for you. That joy and relief come out in Charles Wesley's hymn "Amazing Love":

> Long my imprisoned spirit lay,
>   fast-bound in sin and nature's night.
> Thine eye diffused a quickening (i.e., life-giving) ray;
> I woke; the dungeon flamed with light.
> My chains fell off, my heart was free,
>   I rose, went forth, and followed thee.

Today under God's mighty and loving rule, the manacles are at long last off your ankles. Yes, you may walk with a permanent limp. But can you learn to give God praise even for that? For today you above all people know on whom you need to lean.

ASSIGNMENTS

1. Meditate on 2 Corinthians 12:9a and list the ways in which you appreciate God's grace to you.

2. If you believe it is right for you to do so, take a "field trip" to a Twelve-Step meeting, whether in your area or in the next town. You may want to go with a friend.

Introductory quotation: Deuteronomy 6:20.

Appendix A—Resource List

The American Self-Help Clearinghouse publishes a useful directory, listing information about all sorts of self-help groups.

American Self-Help Clearinghouse
Saint Clares-Riverside Medical Center
Denville, NJ 07834
(201) 625-7101

The easiest way to get in touch with a recovery group is to look for a local number in your telephone directory. Or you may contact the national headquarters, and they will mail you some literature and a list of local meetings.

Al-Anon/Alateen Family Group
  Headquarters
PO Box 862, Midtown Station
New York, NY 10018
800–356–9996

Alcoholics Anonymous
PO Box 459, Grand Central
  Station
New York, NY 10163
(212) 870–3400

Alcoholics Victorious [Christian]
9370 S.W. Greenburg Road
Suite 411
Tigard, OR 97323
(503) 245–9629

Cocaine Anonymous
6125 Washington Blvd.
Suite 202
Los Angeles, CA 90230
(213) 559–5833

Debtors Anonymous
PO Box 20322
New York, NY 10025
(212) 642–8222

Emotions Anonymous
PO Box 4245
St. Paul, MN 55104
(612) 647–9712

Gamblers Anonymous
PO Box 17173
Los Angeles, CA 90017
(213) 386–8789

Messies Anonymous [not Twelve-
Step; Christian orientation]
5025 S.W. 114th Ave.
Miami, FL 33165
(305) 271–8404

Narcotics Anonymous
PO Box 9999
Van Nuys, CA 91409
(818) 780–3951

Nicotine Anonymous
2118 Greenwich St.
San Francisco, CA 94123
(415) 922–8575

Overcomers Outreach
  [Christian]
2290 W. Whittier Blvd.
Suite A/D
La Habra, CA 90631
(310) 697–3994

Overeaters Anonymous
PO Box 44020
Rio Rancho, NM 87174-4020
(505) 891–2664

Overeaters Victorious [Christian]
PO Box 2330
Orange, CA 92669

Sexaholics Anonymous
PO Box 300
Simi Valley, CA 93062
(818) 704–9854

Sex Addicts Anonymous
PO Box 3038
Minneapolis, MN 55403
(612) 339–0217

Sex and Love Addicts
  Anonymous
PO Box 119, New Town Branch
Boston, MA 02258
(617) 332–1845

Substance Abusers Victorious
  [Christian]
One Cascade Plaza
Akron, OH 44308

Workaholics Anonymous
PO Box 661501
Los Angeles, CA 90066
(310) 859–5804

Appendix B—
The Twelve Steps and
Twelve Traditions of A. A.

The Twelve Steps

1. We admitted we were powerless over alcohol—that our lives had become unmanageable.
2. Came to believe that a Power greater than ourselves could restore us to sanity.
3. Made a decision to turn our will and our lives over to the care of God as we understood Him.
4. Made a searching and fearless moral inventory of ourselves.
5. Admitted to God, to ourselves and to another human being the exact nature of our wrongs.
6. Were entirely ready to have God remove all these defects of character.
7. Humbly asked Him to remove our short-comings.
8. Made a list of all persons we had harmed, and became willing to make amends to them all.
9. Made direct amends to such people wherever possible, except when to do so would injure them or others.
10. Continued to take personal inventory, and when we were wrong, promptly admitted it.
11. Sought through prayer and meditation to improve our conscious contact with God as we understood Him, praying only for knowledge of His will for us and the power to carry that out.
12. Having had a spiritual awakening as the result of these steps, we tried to carry this message to alcoholics and to practice these principles in all our affairs.

The Twelve Traditions

1. Our common welfare should come first; personal recovery depends upon A. A. unity.
2. For our group purpose there is but one ultimate authority—a loving God as He may express Himself in our group conscience. Our leaders are but trusted servants; they do not govern.
3. The only requirement for A. A. membership is a desire to stop drinking.
4. Each group should be autonomous except in matters affecting other groups or A. A. as a whole.
5. Each group has but one primary purpose—to carry its message to the alcoholic who still suffers.
6. An A. A. group ought never endorse, finance, or lend the A. A. name to any related facility or outside enterprise, lest problems of money, property, and prestige divert us from our primary purpose.
7. Every A. A. group ought to be fully self-supporting, declining outside contributions.
8. Alcoholics Anonymous should remain forever nonprofessional, but our service centers may employ special workers.
9. A. A. as such, ought never be organized; but we may create service boards or committees directly responsible to those they serve.
10. Alcoholics Anonymous has no opinion on outside issues; hence the A. A. name ought never be drawn into public controversy.
11. Our public relations policy is based on attraction rather than promotion; we need always maintain personal anonymity at the level of press, radio, and films.
12. Anonymity is the spiritual foundation of our traditions, ever reminding us to place principles before personalities.

List of Works Cited

Alcoholics Anonymous World Services (A. A.). 1976. *Alcoholics Anonymous.* 3d ed. New York: A. A. World Services.

Augustine. 1961. *Confessions.* Trans. R. S. Pine-Coffin. New York: Penguin.

Berger, G. 1992. *Addiction.* Rev. ed. New York: Franklin Watts.

Homer. 1944. *The Odyssey of Homer.* Trans. Samuel Butler. Roslyn, N.Y.: Walter J. Black.

Nakken, C. 1988. *The Addictive Personality.* San Francisco: Harper/Hazeldon.

Sykes, C. 1992. *A Nation of Victims.* New York: St. Martin.

Washton, A. and D. Boundy. 1989. *Willpower's Not Enough.* New York: HarperCollins.

White, B. and E. Madara, eds. 1992. *The Self-Help Sourcebook.* 4th ed. Denville, N.J.: American Self-Help Clearinghouse.

Wilson, J. and J. Wilson, eds. 1992. *Addictionary.* New York: Fireside/Parkside.

Wright, J., ed. 1994. *The Universal Almanac 1994.* Kansas City: Andrews & McMeel.

For Further Reading

Al-Anon Family Groups. *Al-Anon Family Groups*. New York: Al-Anon Family Group Headquarters, 1986. The Al-Anon program in one small book: the steps and traditions, personal stories, the dynamics of Al-Anon meetings, how to start a local group.

————. *Al-Anon's Twelve Steps & Twelve Traditions*. New York: Al-Anon Family Group Headquarters, 1986. Al-Anon's version of A. A.'s 12+12. The brief chapters all contain "Thinking It Over" sections and a personal story to illustrate the point.

————. *Alateen—Hope for Children of Alcoholics*. New York: Al-Anon Family Group Headquarters, Inc., 1981. Easy to digest sections on Alcoholism, the Twelve Steps, the Twelve Traditions, and Personal Stories. Useful introduction to teens or to those who don't want to wade through A. A. literature.

Alcoholics Anonymous World Services. *Alcoholics Anonymous*. 3d ed. New York: A. A. World Services, 1976. The "Bible" of the Twelve-Step movement. Written in 1938–39 by Bill Wilson, co-founder of A. A. Must reading.

————. *Twelve Steps and Twelve Traditions*. New York: A. A. World Services, 1952. Written anonymously by Bill Wilson, co-founder of A. A. Short chapters expound the Steps and the Twelve Traditions, the principles by which A. A. is run. The 12+12 is a standard A. A. tool.

Allison, Patricia and Jack Yost. *Hooked—but not Helpless: Ending Your Love/Hate Relationship with Nicotine*. Portland, OR: BridgeCity Books, 1990. Easy to read manual applying rational-emotive therapy to smoking.

Beattie, Melody. *Codependent No More: How to Stop Controlling Others and Start Caring for Yourself.* New York: Hazeldon Books, Harper & Row, 1987. One of the most popular books on a popular theme. Beattie deals with the control and over-involvement associated with being close to an addict. She has written a number of books on this theme.

Berman, Linda and Mary-Ellen Siegel. *Behind the 8-Ball: A Guide for Families of Gamblers.* New York: A Fireside/Parkside Recovery Book, 1992. Superb book with much detailed information for those who love a gambler. There is advice on managing family finances when a spouse is a gambler.

Carnes, Patrick. *Out of the Shadows: Understanding Sexual Addiction.* 2d. ed. Minneapolis, MN: CompCare Publishers, 1992. This book comes highly recommended by people in the field, and it gives a thorough and detailed overview of the problem. His solution is to alter one's "core values" in order to change.

Coleman, Sally and Nancy Hull-Mast. *Can't Buy Me Love: Freedom from Compulsive Spending and Money Obsession.* Minneapolis, MN: CompCare Publishers, 1992. A warm and practical book. Includes worksheets for the addict and help for the family. Also includes material on "poverty addiction."

Fish, Melinda. *When Addiction Comes to Church: Helping Yourself and Others Move into Recovery.* Old Tappan, NJ: Chosen Books, 1990. She combines biblical truths with ideas about self-esteem, and promotes starting church support groups with a Christian version of the Steps.

Friends in Recovery. *The Twelve Steps for Christians from Addictive and Other Dysfunctional Families.* San Diego: Recovery Publications, Inc., 1988. It is "based on biblical teachings" and there are some biblical passages along with the Twelve Steps. There is a workbook as well, *The Twelve Steps—A Spiritual Journey.* From the same publisher, see also the book by Martin Davis, *The Gospel and the Twelve Steps: Developing a Closer Relationship with Jesus* (1993).

Gamblers Anonymous. *Sharing Recovery through Gamblers Anonymous.* Los Angeles: Gamblers Anonymous, 1984. It gives a description of compulsive gambling, a long composite case study, and a description of the GA "Unity Program" of recovery. Also includes a survey of GA members.

Hart, Archibald. *Healing Life's Hidden Addictions: overcoming the closet compulsions that waste your time and control your life.* Ann Arbor, Michigan: Servant Publications, 1990. Closet addictions include shopping, sex, worry. He roots some of these in our society of self-indulgence and our need to relieve boredom. His solutions are stress reduction, cognitive restructuring, higher frustration level, etc. Not distinctly Christian, but with a few verses as examples.

Keller, Ron. *Twelve Steps to a New Day: An Interactive Recovery Workbook for Spiritual Growth.* Nashville: Thomas Nelson Publishers, 1993. "The Twelve-Step lifestyle is for everyone," the book advertises. He offers biblical applications of the steps for a small group study. His model deals with any issue—marriage problems, nicotine, adult children of alcoholics, etc.

Killinger, Barbara. *Workaholics: The Respectable Addicts.* New York: Fireside Books, 1991. Some good material about what workaholics look like and how their families can cope. She discusses how workaholics are afraid that they are really lazy, bound to be found out as losers, etc.

Lee, Jimmy Ray. *Living Free: A Christ-centered Twelve-Step Program.* Grand Rapids: Baker Books, 1993. An adaptation of the Twelve Steps for evangelical recovery support groups. Includes a workbook and guidelines for group leaders. This book is more oriented to the Bible than are many Christian recovery books.

Maloney, Michael and Rachel Kranz. *Straight Talk about Eating Disorders.* New York: Facts on File, 1991. Some good information about eating disorders, including compulsive eating. Clearly and succinctly written with relevant statistics. Geared mainly for teens and their parents.

Martin, Grant. *When Good Things Become Addictions: Gaining Freedom from Our Compulsions.* Wheaton, IL: Victor Books, 1990. Formerly titled *Regaining Control.* He has some thoughts on how good things (romance, relationships, sex, food, power, religion, activity) take over our lives. The section on eating disorders is insightful. He tries to integrate psychology with the Scriptures.

Minirth, Frank, and Paul Meier, et al. *Love Hunger: Recovery from Food Addiction.* Nashville: Thomas Nelson, 1990. The extremely popular Minirth-Meier books are not specifically oriented to the Bible or to a God-centered universe. This book favors the OA program, and argues that the cause of overeating is emotional and spiritual deprivation. Other books from the Minirth-Meier team: Robert Hemfelt, Minirth, and Meier, *Love Is a Choice: Recovery for Codependent Relationships* (1989), which contains conventional co-dependency ideas with a tiny sprinkling of references to the Bible. *The Path to Serenity* by Hemfelt, Fowler, Minirth, and Meier (1991) is somewhat more oriented to finding the God of the Bible. *Steps to a New Beginning: Leading Others to Christ through the Twelve Step Process* by Sam Shoemaker, Frank Minirth and others (1993) is an attempt at a Christian understanding of the Twelve Steps.

Mooney, Al J., Arlene Eisenberg, and Howard Eisenberg. *The Recovery Book*. New York: Workman Publishing, 1992. A massive book with information and resources for almost every recovery topic. Written with clarity and style.

Mundis, Jerrold. *How to Get Out of Debt, Stay Out of Debt & Live Prosperously*. New York: Bantam Books, 1988. Based on the Debtors Anonymous Twelve-Step program, it is full of useful and interesting material. His understanding of spirituality is very vague, and consists in large part in affirming your own worth and visualizing what you want to be real. His main goal in achieving financial stability is having more money to spend.

Overeaters Anonymous World Service. *Overeaters Anonymous*. Torrance, CA: Overeaters Anonymous, 1980. Known as the Brown Book. A brief description of the program introduces these 30 stories of recovery from OA.

————. *The Twelve Steps and Twelve Traditions of Overeaters Anonymous*. Torrance, CA: Overeaters Anonymous, 1993. The equivalent to A. A.'s 12+12 from the OA perspective.

Shoemaker, Samuel M. *Courage to Change: the Christian Roots of the 12-Step Movement*. Compiled and edited by Bill Pittman and Dick B. Grand Rapids: Fleming H. Revell, 1994. If you've ever wondered why aspects of A. A. sound so Christian, this is the book for you. The editors trace the influence of Eylscopal minister Sam Schumaker and the evangelical Oxford Group upon A. A. founder Bill Wilson. Shoemaker's many published books are highlighted as the foundation of the Steps and the Big Book. This is a remarkable work, and should be read by every Christian in a Twelve-Step group.

Stephens, Larry D. *Please Let Me Know You God: How to Restore a True Image of God and Experience His Love Again*. Nashville: Thomas Nelson Publishers, 1993. He stresses finding the God of truth in the Bible, and that our feelings must not color who God truly is. He also shows that while God allows evil to happen, he makes no mistakes.

Washton, Arnold, and Donna Boundy. *Willpower's Not Enough: Understanding and Recovering from Addictions of Every Kind*. New York: HarperCollins Publishers, 1989. Some helpful insights, particularly on avoiding relapse and recovering if you do fall.

Wilson, Jan R. and Judith A. Wilson. *Addictionary: A Primer of Recovery Terms and Concepts from Abstinence to Withdrawal*. New York: A Fireside/Parkside Recovery Book, 1992. A remarkably useful, balanced reference tool, breaking the jargon into plain terms. They list addresses for recovery and resource groups.

Recovery Devotional Guides

Of the dozens of the daily devotional books, most impose the Twelve Steps and conventional psychology onto a wide variety of verses. Those with mixed messages include *Another Day of Grace* (by Morreim, who says God is BEST revealed in Christ, Augsburg), and *God Grant* (Keller, HarperCollins).

Much better are the brief thoughts in *The Bible Promise Life Recovery Devotional: A Promise Each Day of Hope, Strength, and Courage* by Wightman Weese (Tyndale House, 1992). This book is more Christ- and cross-centered than one usually finds, although it partakes of the disease model of addiction.

And what about the *Life Recovery Bible* (executive editors Stephen F. Arterburn and David A. Stoop, from Tyndale House, 1992)? Based on the Living Bible, it contains Twelve Step Devotionals, Recovery Notes, Serenity Prayer Devotionals, chain studies, studies on Bible personalities. You will find some fine insights, but it has the same weakness of the devotionals—they read topics into verses where they do not truly belong. On the other hand, you can give it to friends in recovery as an introduction to the Bible. On the whole, however, we recommend that you simply buy a Bible in a readable translation and see what is there for yourself.

Furthermore . . . it is recommended that you do not limit your reading to recovery manuals. They parrot each other, and they tend to have the same fuzzy image of God. The works of Sinclair Ferguson, J. I. Packer, or Jerry Bridges will give steady and practical help for the Christian. And

105

since recovery books may fall into the snare of trendiness, you might enjoy some books that have stood the test of time. These classics are short (nearly all around 100 pages), entertaining, and readily available:

From the seventeenth century, John Bunyan's *Pilgrim's Progress* is a description of the Christian life through the story of a journey to the Celestial City. A much longer book of Bunyan's that describes the battle with Satan in terms of a siege against the city of Mansoul is *The Holy War.* Happily, both books are available in modern paraphrased versions.

C. S. Lewis' books are also helpful. *Perelandra* (1944), the second volume of his science fiction fantasy, is chock full of insights about God, Satan, humanity, good and evil. *The Great Divorce* (1952) is a tale of a journey from Hell to Heaven on which you learn about the stickiness of evil. *Screwtape Letters* (1943) is a fictional set of correspondence from a demon high in Satan's bureaucracy to a low-level tempter.

Also recommended is J. B. Phillips, *Your God Is too Small* (1953). If you don't think that God can help you, perhaps your perception of him is mistaken. Phillips shows that there is no use in trying to conquer adult problems with a nursery school theology.

And lastly, you might try that legendary work by Robert Louis Stevenson, *The Strange Case of Dr. Jekyll and Mr. Hyde* (1886). Thought by many to be an allegory of drug addiction, this classic tale explores how chemicals unleash the evil that lies within us. Don't settle for the Hollywood revisions!

Endnotes

Chapter 1: *A Kingdom of Slaves*

1. Rom. 7:18b–19, 23b.
* All the characters in this book are composites, and are not intended to represent any individuals, living or dead.
2. Prov. 23:29–35.
3. Jer. 10:10a.
4. Heb. 3:12.
5. Ps. 42:11.

Chapter 2: *The Real Nature of the Kingdom of Slaves*

1. Rom. 5:12.
2. 2 Tim. 3:2–5 (italics mine).
3. Mark 12:30.
4. Gen. 1:27.
5. 1 Cor. 6:19b–20.

Chapter 3: *Finding Freedom in the Kingdom of God*

1. 1 Thess. 1:9b–10 (italics mine).
2. 1 Cor. 6:9–11a.
3. Eph. 5:18a.
4. 1 Cor. 6:11b (italics mine).
5. 1 Cor. 2:2.
6. Rom. 6:11–12.
7. Rom. 6:13a, 16.
8. 2 Pet. 2:19b.

9. Rom. 6:13b.
10. Titus 2:11–12 (italics mine).
11. Rom. 6:19b.
12. Rom. 12:1.
13. Col. 1:29b.
14. James 4:8.

Chapter 4: *Counterattacks of the Dark Kingdom*

1. Matt. 6:34.
2. 1 Pet. 4:7.
3. Matt. 6:27.
4. 1 Pet. 5:5b–9a.
5. Luke 4:12.
6. James 4:8a.
7. Eph. 4:27.
8. Gal. 5:13.
9. 1 John 1:9.
10. Rom. 5:1b.

Chapter 5: *Living at Peace in the Kingdom of God*

1. Ps. 139:1–4.
2. Matt. 5:23–24.
3. Eph. 4:28.
4. Matt. 18:15.
5. Heb. 10:24–25.
6. 1 Cor. 4:7.
7. 1 Pet. 3:8.

Chapter 6: *Ongoing Life in the Kingdom of God*

1. Gal. 6:1–5.
2. Eph. 5:17–18.
3. Eph. 2:3–5.
4. 2 Cor. 12:9a.